ALSO BY BURTON G. MALKIEL

A Random Walk Down Wall Street

Global Bargain Hunting:
The Investor's Guide to Profits
in Emerging Markets
(WITH J. P. MEI)

Expectations and the Structure of Share Prices
(WITH JOHN G. CRAGG)

Strategies and Rational Decisions in the
Securities Options Market
(WITH RICHARD E. QUANDT)

Winning Investment Strategies

THE INDEX

A STEP-BY-STEP

RICHARD E. EVANS

FUND SOLUTION

INVESTOR'S GUIDE

Introduction and a New Look at Index Funds by

Burton G. Malkiel

A FIRESIDE BOOK
PUBLISHED BY SIMON & SCHUSTER
NEW YORK LONDON TORONTO SYDNEY SINGAPORE

FIRESIDE
Rockefeller Center
1230 Avenue of the Americas
New York, NY 10020

Designed by Ruth Lee
Manufactured in the United States of America

10 9 8 7 6 5 4 3 2 1
The Library of Congress has cataloged the Simon & Schuster edition as
follows:

Evans, Richard, E. (Richard Eli), 1937–
    Earn more (sleep better) : the index fund solution / Richard E. Evans and
    Burton G. Malkiel.
        p.   cm.
        1. Index mutual funds. I. Malkiel, Burton Gordon. II. Title.
    HG4530.E93 1999
    332.63'27—dc21   98-42001
                                                          CIP

ISBN 0-684-85250-0
        0-684-86596-3 (Pbk)

To my wife, Faith,
without whom not.
　　　　　　—R.E.E.

ACKNOWLEDGMENTS

JOHN C. BOGLE, CHAIRMAN OF THE BOARD AND FOUNDER, THE Vanguard Group, champion of index funds and creator of the first and largest public index fund.

Rodney Alldredge and George Daniels (Daniels & Alldredge, Birmingham Alabama), who have demonstrated the advantages of global indexing in risk-controlled portfolios.

Dr. Harry Markowitz, Noble Laureate and prime mover in the development of Modern Portfolio Theory, which (among other things) set the stage for successful indexing.

R. T. Whitman (Director, KPMG Acumen, Short Hills, New Jersey), who has led the industry in developing low-cost personalized financial planning.

RICHARD E. EVANS
Hastings-on-Hudson, New York
index-info@mindspring.com

Author's note: mathematics reviewed in part by Steven S. Guo, Ph.D., Clark University, Worcester, Massachusetts.

CONTENTS

INTRODUCTION

THIS IS LIKELY TO BE THE MOST IMPORTANT BOOK YOU WILL EVER read about investing. It recommends a very simple, step-by-step strategy for individual investors to do what some of the most sophisticated professionals do—use index funds as the vehicle of choice for their investment assets. Simply stated, index funds consist of the stocks in a broad stock market index, such as the Standard and Poor's 500 Stock Index or the even broader Wilshire 5000 Index. Index investing is thus nothing more than a strategy of buying and holding all, or a representative sample, of these stocks. Sure, it's a plain vanilla investment in an era when the more exotic flavors are highly touted by the leading investment magazines and many brokers. But this simple investment strategy has outperformed all but a tiny handful of the thousands of equity mutual funds that are sold to the public. Readers who follow the advice in these pages are likely to earn more from their investments while sleeping better as their returns become more predictable.

I have been a fan of index funds for more than twenty-five years. I first recommended them in 1973 in the first edition of my book *A Random Walk Down Wall Street*. In fact, in 1973, index funds were not available for the public—they were then only used by a few institutional investors such as the big pension funds. The first publicly available index fund was started in 1976. I said then, as I say now, that index investing is a sure strategy to gain investment returns that exceed those available from the average mutual fund, which is constantly in the market actively buying and selling stocks in a futile attempt to gain extraordinary returns.

HOW HAS
INDEXING PERFORMED?

How has the indexing strategy fared over the past quarter of a century? The answer is very well indeed. The graph on page 15 shows the proportion of actively managed equity mutual funds that have failed to match the broad Wilshire 5000 stock index— an index made up of essentially all the stocks in the S&P 500 (an index heavily weighted by the largest U.S. corporations) and a large number (more than 4,500) of smaller firms. The exhibit shows that there have been very few years when even half of the actively managed funds have been able to beat the index. About two-thirds of the actively managed funds are outperformed by the index in a typical year. On average, the typical actively managed fund underperforms the index by about two percentage points a year. And that calculation ignores the sales charges that are imposed by some actively managed funds and the extra taxes an investor pays on funds that turn over their portfolios rapidly. Throughout this book, my co-author Richard Evans prefers to call actively managed funds "non-index" funds. His point, which is entirely accurate, is that index funds also need active attention to ensure that they continue to mirror the index they are designed to represent. But what index funds don't do is try to select a portfolio of individual securities that the non-index man-

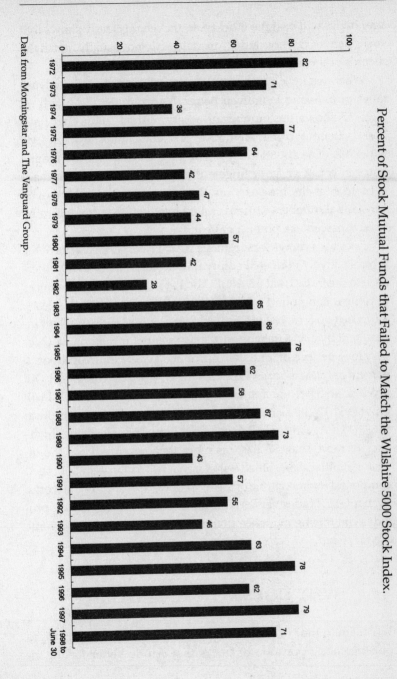

Percent of Stock Mutual Funds that Failed to Match the Wilshire 5000 Stock Index.

Data from Morningstar and The Vanguard Group.

ager hopes will beat the index. And the record clearly shows that such "active" or "non-index" managers do not usually match the records of the market as a whole.

When we look at returns over a ten-year period, the advantages of indexing look even better. For example, the graph on page 17 shows the number of equity mutual funds that have done better or worse than the S&P 500 Stock Index between 1988 and 1997. (The situation is similar for the Wilshire 5000 Index.) You can count on your fingers the number of funds that managed to beat the index by any meaningful amount. Moreover, substantial numbers of funds failed to meet the index return by several percentage points per year.

Does the average 2-percentage point underperformance of the typical actively managed equity mutual fund make a real difference to the individual investor? You bet it does! Small differences in returns compound into enormous differences over the years. Suppose you are a twenty-year-old who puts aside $10,000 for investment in stocks to be used at age seventy for retirement. Over very long periods of time stocks produce a gross return of about 10 percent per year, so after expenses the typical active manager will produce an 8 percent annual return. Over fifty years, $10,000 will grow to $1,174,000 if it earns 10 percent per year. But it will grow to $469,000 if it earns only 8 percent per year. The staggering difference of more than $700,000 is more than seventy times the investor's initial stake. Small wonder that Albert Einstein described compound interest as one of the most powerful forces in the world. In chapter 5, "Index versus Non-Index Fund Returns," Evans provides convincing evidence that index investors do indeed come out far ahead.

WHY DOES INDEXING WORK?

Why should indexing work? Why should a computer be able to put together a portfolio of stocks that can do better for the in-

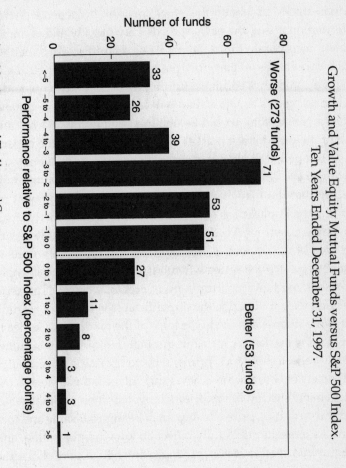

Growth and Value Equity Mutual Funds versus S&P 500 Index.
Ten Years Ended December 31, 1997.

Data from Morningstar and The Vanguard Group.

vestor than one selected by intelligent, well-trained, and highly paid experts? There are four reasons.

First, there is considerable evidence that our securities markets are extremely efficient in digesting information about individual stocks or about the stock market in general. When information arises, the news spreads very quickly and is immediately incorporated into the prices of securities. Thus, neither technical analysis (of past price patterns) nor fundamental analysis (of a company's earnings, future prospects, and so on, to determine a stock's proper value) will help an investor to achieve returns greater than would be obtained by buying and holding one of the broad stock market indices. It is not that the experts are incompetent. Rather, it is precisely because professionals are so diligent in continuously examining stock prices for any mispricing that the market always reflects their best judgment regarding the implications of all information that is known.

This efficient-market theory, as it is known, is associated with the idea of a "random walk," which is a term loosely used to characterize a price series where all subsequent price changes represent random departures from previous prices. The term was first used to describe the unpredictable behavior of a drunk left in the middle of a field. The logic of the random-walk idea is not that the market is capricious but that if information is immediately reflected in stock prices, then tomorrow's price change will reflect only tomorrow's news and will be independent of the price changes today. But real news is by definition unpredictable, and thus resulting price changes must be unpredictable and random. As a result, prices fully reflect all known information, and even uninformed investors buying a diversified portfolio at the tableau of prices given by the market will obtain a rate of return as good as that achieved by the experts. The way I put it in my book *A Random Walk Down Wall Street*, a blindfolded chimpanzee throwing darts at the *Wall Street Journal* could select a portfolio that would do as well as the experts. Of course I didn't literally suggest that investors should throw darts, but rather that they

"Dilbert" reprinted by permission of United Feature Syndicate, Inc.

should simply buy and hold a large group of stocks that represented the stock market as a whole. In other words, investors would be well served by buying an index fund.

The second reason that indexing works is because it is so cost efficient. The typical expense level for managing a public index fund is .2 percent (two-tenths of one percent) per year. Actively managed funds have a typical expense level of 1.5 percent and many of these funds have even higher expenses. Since professional portfolio managers dominate stock trading activity (most individuals own their stocks through funds), the experts as a whole cannot do any better than the whole market—*they are the market*. This would be true even if the stock market were highly inefficient. Hence if active managers charge well over 1 percent per year in extra expenses, they must then underperform an index fund that buys the whole market by an equivalent amount.

A third reason why indexing outperforms managed funds is that the funds incur heavy trading expenses. The typical actively managed fund sells almost all the securities in the portfolio each year, replacing them with other stocks. Indeed, many funds turn over their entire portfolio more than once each year. But this portfolio turnover is expensive. The fund pays brokerage charges on each transaction as well as the security dealer's spread between buying and selling prices. The fund also pays a "market impact" cost. When it buys a stock it tends to drive up its price, making the purchase more expensive. When it sells it tends to drive the price down, reducing the fund's net proceeds. These trading costs can easily amount to between .5 percent and 1 percent per year. The index fund, on the other hand, simply holds on to its securities from year to year and thus largely avoids these transaction charges. Between extra professional portfolio management fees and trading costs, the active manager would have to outperform the index by 1.5 to 2 percentage points per year to produce net returns that just matched the index. No wonder that the typical performance gap between the experts and an index fund has generally been within the above range.

But the fourth and perhaps biggest advantage of indexing for the taxable investor lies in its tax advantage of deferring the realization of capital gains or avoiding them completely if the shares are later bequeathed. To the extent that the long-run uptrend in stock prices continues, switching from security to security involves realizing capital gains that are subject to tax. Taxes are a crucially important financial consideration since the earlier realization of capital gains will substantially reduce net returns, as Evans shows in chapter 14. Index funds do not trade from security to security and, thus, they tend to avoid capital gains taxes.

Stock trading among institutional investors is like an isometric exercise: Lots of energy is expended, but between one investment manager and another it all balances out, and the transaction costs incurred by the managers detract from performance. The other big detractor from performance is fund expenses. As Don Phillips, the president of the Morningstar mutual-fund rating service, has said, "If you pay the executive at Sara Lee more, it doesn't make the cheesecake less good. But with mutual funds, it comes directly out of the batter." Moreover, the biggest advantage of indexing for the taxable investor lies in its advantage of deferring or avoiding capital gains taxes.

Some critics of indexing argue that the strategy is one of "guaranteed mediocrity." It is certainly true that the index-fund investor gives up the chance of boasting to one's golfing partners about the fantastic gains made by picking stock-market winners. But experience conclusively shows that index-fund buyers obtain results exceeding those of the typical fund managers whose large advisory fees and substantial portfolio turnover tend to reduce investment returns. I am convinced that most investors—both individual and institutional—will find the guarantee of playing the stock-market game at par every round a very attractive one.

WHY NOT BUY JUST THE SUPERIOR PERFORMING FUNDS?

There is no doubt that some mutual-fund managers have been able to beat the market—a few by significant amounts. This fact suggests an obvious strategy: Invest only in those funds with superior long-term records. The financial press is happy to help out by singing the praises of particular portfolio managers who recently have produced well above average returns. There is only one problem with that strategy. Good performance in one period does not predict good performance in the next. As long as there are averages, some managers will beat them. Undoubtedly, some actively managed funds will substantially beat the market in the years to come. The problem is that investors have no way of knowing in advance who those superior managers will be, as Evans shows in chapter 6, "Does the Past Predict?"

I have put the records of all mutual funds on the computer and attempted to find a strategy that would enable an investor to select the best ones. I tried a strategy of buying only those funds that had the best record over the past year, or the past two, five, or ten years. I tried a strategy of buying only those funds favored by the financial magazines or investment services, such as the "honor roll funds" selected by *Forbes* magazine or the "five-star" funds chosen by Morningstar mutual fund service. While some of these strategies worked for some periods during the late 1970s and early 1980s, none of these strategies were successful over the long run in consistently picking funds that could either beat the market or even do better than the average equity mutual fund. As Nobel laureate in economics Paul Samuelson has stated, "Investors would be well advised to avoid looking for such tiny needles in such large haystacks." The chances of identifying the very few managers who will beat the market are close to nil.

SURVIVORSHIP BIAS AND MUTUAL FUNDS RETURNS

In 1997 I appeared on a public television program with Peter Lynch, the legendary former manager of the Magellan Fund, a fund with a superb long-term record. Lynch was asked why the average money manager has underperformed the S&P 500. He replied flatly, "That's just not true ... the average mutual fund has beaten the market for twenty-five years, it's beaten it for thirty-five years, it's beaten it for, I think, fifteen years. It has not beaten it for five (years)." In short, Lynch admitted that the mid-1990s were not stunning years for active portfolio managers, but he claimed that during the 1980s and in earlier decades, the pros' records were superb.

There is a certain sense in which Lynch's statement is true, but only if one ignores what statisticians call "survivorship bias." If one looks only at the funds with twenty-five-year records, one is, in effect, looking at funds that survived for twenty-five years. But only the successful funds survive. Funds that do poorly are very difficult to sell and tend to get merged into more successful funds in the mutual-fund complex so that their bad records get buried. Thus, if you look only at the performance of funds with twenty-five-year records, you will tend to see an unrealistically rosy picture of the success of fund management. The problem is that the investor cannot know in advance which funds will be successful and therefore which funds will survive.

A numerical calculation will illustrate the difference between surviving and nonsurviving funds during the 1980s, a period when Peter Lynch claimed that active portfolio managers out-performed the S&P 500 Stock Index. Taking all mutual funds with an objective of capital appreciation that existed at the start of 1982 and survived through 1991, I found that their average rate of return was 18.1 percent, comfortably above the S&P 500 return of 17.5 percent for the same period. This is the kind of comparison you would make if you asked what was the average annual return for all such funds existing on January 1, 1992, that had at least a ten-year record. (I do the calculation up to the start of 1992 because Lynch did admit that the pros as a group did poorly after 1992.) So it appears that Lynch was correct.

But if we examine the average fund returns for *all* funds with a capital appreciation objective existing during the 1980s irre-spective of whether they survived for ten years or not, we get a different result. When we figure the average fund return for the decade, we include all funds existing during every year of the period, including those funds that didn't make it all the way through 1991. Now we find that the average fund return was only 16.3 percent, well below the 18.1 percent return of the sur-vivors and also well below the 17.5 percent return of the S&P 500. The differences are even more dramatic for the fifteen-year pe-riod ending December 31, 1991. The average return for equity funds surviving over the whole fifteen-year period was 18.7 per-cent per annum. The average yearly return for *all* funds, includ-ing nonsurvivors, was only 14.5 percent.

I have done similar analysis for "growth and income" funds as well as for all equity funds, whatever their stated objective. The results are the same. Analyses that exclude nonsurviving funds will significantly overstate the returns received by mutual fund investors. This is the error Peter Lynch makes when he claims that the average mutual fund has outperformed the S&P index. The facts remain that the average manager significantly underperforms the index and has done so not only over the past five years, but over the past ten, fifteen, and twenty-five years as well.

ARE BIGGER FUNDS BETTER
THAN SMALLER ONES?

One of the reasons even the successful actively managed fund fails to maintain any advantage over an index fund is that as the fund grows in size, it gets harder and harder to manage the portfolio. Investors should remember that many of the best long-run performing mutual funds attained their excellent records when they were small. Indeed, some fund complexes will start a number of "incubator" funds and continue to market only those that have succeeded. For example, suppose ten funds are initiated and three are successful in beating the market. Those three survive and the other seven are merged into more successful funds, thus burying their poor records. Of course, the long-run rates of return of these three successful funds will reflect the early years of superior performance.

There are several reasons why larger size tends to inhibit performance. First, small funds can benefit from a strategic placement of new issues in the fund. A mutual fund complex might concentrate its allocation of a hot initial public offering in a very small fund, thus boosting performance substantially. A multibillion-dollar fund has no such opportunity since the effect of a new issue's stock-price appreciation is likely to get lost in the rounding.

A second reason large size may inhibit performance is that the universe of securities available for the fund's portfolio decreases with size. Mutual funds usually operate with two constraints. First, they will want to limit the holdings of any individual security in their portfolio to at most 2 percent to 5 percent of their total portfolio to maintain adequate diversification. Second, they will usually be unwilling to hold positions representing more than 5 percent to 10 percent of the firm's outstanding shares to ensure adequate liquidity should the fund wish to sell the shares. Together, these constraints sharply limit the number of companies available for investment.

Suppose one mutual fund has $1 billion in assets and decides that to maintain adequate diversification it will hold fifty securities, putting 2 percent of the portfolio ($20 million) in each individual stock. Suppose, further, that the fund decides it does not want to hold more than 5 percent of the value of any one company. John Bogle, the founder of The Vanguard Group, has estimated that 1,850 stocks would be available for investment by the fund. Now suppose the fund grows to $20 billion and operates with the same constraints. Limiting itself to no more than 5 percent of a firm's total capitalization will reduce the number of available securities by more than tenfold to 182 companies. In other words, growing from $1 billion to $20 billion in size is likely to reduce the number of securities available for purchase by as much as 90 percent.

A third reason size makes performance more difficult is that transaction costs increase with size. While big institutions can trade at pennies per share in brokerage commissions, moving substantial blocks of securities around tends to move market prices. The funds will be able to take on a large position only at a premium from going market prices and to liquidate that position only at a discount. Moreover, since other funds (and other accounts) in the complex are likely to take on similar stock positions, the effects are likely to be larger than would be the case if the funds were independent. While reliable studies of transactions costs do not exist, most professionals recognize that they are potentially quite substantial. According to a study by the Plexus Group, typical trading costs for investment managers may be as large as .8 percent of the dollar amount of a transaction involving a sale and purchase. And the trading costs of larger funds are likely to be substantially higher than for smaller funds.

The records of two of the most successful mutual funds will illustrate the tendency of superior performance to disappear as the size of the fund increases. The graph on page 26 shows the performance of the "Around the World Fund," which is the Magellan Fund, the largest equity mutual fund and a stellar long-run

"Around the World Fund" versus S&P 500 Index.*

Three-Year Rolling Performance (Annualized).
The vertical bars show the percentage point gains (losses)
of the fund versus the S&P 500 Stock Index.

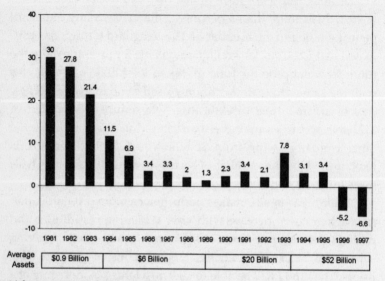

| Average Assets | $0.9 Billion | $6 Billion | $20 Billion | $52 Billion |

*After expenses of 0.2 percent.

Source: Updated from John C. Bogle, " 'Be Not the First . . . Nor Yet the Last': Six Things to Remember About Indexing, and One to Forget," 1996 Association for Investment Management and Research Conference, May 8, 1996.

performer. In the early years of the fund, when its assets were less than a billion dollars, performance was particularly outstanding. The fund beat the market over three-year periods in the late 1970s and early 1980s by 20 to 30 percentage points per year. Note, however, that the excess performance during the remainder of the 1980s and into the 1990s, while certainly impressive, was substantially lower than in the earlier periods. The exhibit shows that the three-year performance through 1996 was substantially worse than the S&P; and in the period ending in 1997, the Magellan Fund was more than 650 basis points (6.5 percentage points) behind the Vanguard Index Trust S&P 500 portfolio, where both returns are calculated after expenses. And the fact that the Magellan Fund charged a load or sales charge on investors entering the fund means that the net returns for investors were even worse.

The graph below shows a similar pattern for the "Alpha Equity Fund," actually the Investment Company of America, the third largest equity mutual fund. (The Vanguard Index Trust S&P 500 Stock portfolio is the second largest equity mutual fund.) When the fund was smaller, its ten-year performance numbers stayed consistently above the S&P 500 index. As the fund grew rapidly during the late 1980s and 1990s, however, performance deteriorated. Bigger is not better when it comes to the profession of managing money. It is important to point out, however, that index funds do not suffer from a size disadvantage. They simply hold on to a market portfolio no matter how large it may get. To the extent the fund grows and new purchases need to be made, they can be done gradually over time through efficient electronic means.

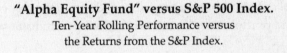

"Alpha Equity Fund" versus S&P 500 Index.
Ten-Year Rolling Performance versus
the Returns from the S&P Index.

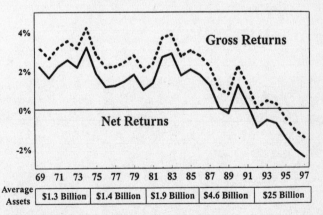

Source: Updated from John C. Bogle, " 'Be Not the First . . . Nor Yet the Last': Six Things to Remember About Indexing, and One to Forget," 1996 Association for Investment Management and Research Conference, May 8, 1996.

A PREVIEW

In the pages that follow, Evans clearly spells out the advantages of index-fund investing. He documents the index advantages of better performance, lower costs, and minimization of taxes. He demonstrates how index funds provide better diversification and more predictability of performance. He also shows the reader how index funds are particularly user-friendly. And he does it all with wit, grace, and clarity.

Readers will find especially helpful Evans's advice on how to build a financial plan and how to construct a portfolio consistent with that plan and with each investor's risk tolerance and particular circumstances. Chapter 10, "Investing for Retirement," covers retirement planning, and it alone is worth far more than the price of this book. Chapter 12 presents enormously helpful advice on taking advantage of all the tax breaks allowed by law. Evans helps ordinary individuals to "invest with confidence." In the final chapter, I put it all together and recommend specific index-fund portfolios for investors in different circumstances.

PART I

Index Funds Versus Non-Index Funds

CHAPTER 1

An Unlikely Beginning

I DID NOT START OUT AS AN ADVOCATE OF INDEX FUNDS. UNTIL RE-cently, I believed there were mutual fund managers who could reliably beat the market. I believed there were market timers who knew when to buy and sell. I believed there were technical analysts who could forecast security prices based on studies of past volume and prices. I believed there were security analysts who could reliably forecast the price of selected stocks.

In short, I believed in the "Great Predictors"—smart, learned investment professionals who could forecast future prices of stocks and bonds.

I felt secure in this belief, based on my twenty-five years of experience in marketing investment products. And why not? A huge industry is based on the premise that there are people who know how to predict the future prices of stocks and bonds. They invest trillions of dollars for the rest of us, who presumably don't have that ability. The Great Predictors include celebrated gurus at mutual fund companies, brokerage firms, banks, and insurance companies—people whose annual compensation may run to over $1 million. These clever, highly paid people couldn't be wrong.

Could they?

THE TURNING POINT

A few years ago, I received a small inheritance. That, plus several IRA rollovers, added up to a significant sum. Of course, I planned to hire professionals to invest my money. But after many years as a corporate manager, I knew it's not smart to delegate a job without some understanding of what you're delegating. So I became a serious student of investing in the stock and bond markets, especially through mutual funds.

My first lesson came from a scholarly book called *The Dow Jones-Irwin Guide to Modern Portfolio Theory* by Robert Hagin. Because the book is now out of print, I'll summarize what I believe to be its major points:

- *The stock and bond markets are "efficient."* As my co-author Burton Malkiel explains in the introduction, this is a technical term referring to the fact that nearly all professional investors work with virtually the same information at the same time. This produces a situation where it is extremely hard for any fund manager to outperform his or her peers for a significant length of time.
- *Technical analysis is worthless to the average investor.* Technical analysis refers to the attempt to forecast security prices based on studies of past volume and prices. Study after study has shown that technical analysis simply doesn't work. It cannot be used to reliably predict stock and bond prices.
- *Fundamental analysis works poorly (if at all) with big-company stocks, and does not work reliably with small-company stocks.* Fun-

damental analysis refers to the process of trying to select securities—and deciding when to buy and sell—based on predicting the future of things that keep changing: the securities markets, the economy, interest rates, the growth rate of industries and companies, and so on. The unexpected looms large.

- *Market timing is an illusion.* After payment of trading costs, there is no system or data set that can reliably predict what the markets will do. Nor can any so-called expert.
- *An investor who buys and holds a diversified portfolio will outperform gurus who move in and out of stocks and bonds.*

Conclusion: It's highly unlikely that any manager can reliably outperform a relevant asset class or "index" (defined in chapter 2). This took me by surprise. How do you explain the fact that many fund managers seem to do it? What about the gurus who tell us the market's going up or going down—and then it does? Yet Hagin's case is compelling. His conclusions aren't based on his opinions, but on the work of economists who compiled and analyzed many years of market behavior. Hagin's bibliography, for example, runs to twenty pages and has 291 listings.

My belief in the possibility of predicting stock and bond prices wavered, but did not disappear. After all, Hagin's book was published in 1979, and a lot has changed since then. Maybe, I thought, Hagin's conclusions are no longer true. Besides, I *wanted* to believe in the Great Predictors. With that in mind, I continued gathering data. I talked with knowledgeable people, spent a lot of time in business libraries, and read extensively. Again and again, I found Hagin's conclusions reinforced by more recent data. When the results are scientifically measured, fund managers, in general, can't do what they say they can do. We're talking about quarterbacks who can't pass and wide receivers who can't catch—but who still collect the big bucks.

Outstanding among the books I consulted were *A Random Walk Down Wall Street* by my co-author and Princeton economist

Burton G. Malkiel, as well as *Bogle on Mutual Funds* by John C. Bogle, founder and chairman of The Vanguard Group. When I called Professor Malkiel with questions about his book, we developed a relationship that eventually led to his becoming co-author of this book. Considering his credentials (rated by *Smart Money* as one of the thirty most influential people in the mutual fund industry, former dean of the Yale School of Management, and member of President Ford's National Council of Economic Advisors), I took his encouragement as a clue that I was on the right track.

Another influential book was *Portfolio Selection* by Nobel laureate Harry Markowitz. He developed a way to assemble different investments to provide the highest return for a given level of risk, based on given set of data. (This is money-in-your-pocket thinking; I'll introduce you to it in chapter 8.)

My reading also included trade periodicals, especially *Institutional Investor, Pensions & Investments,* and *Plan Sponsor.* Personal finance publications included *Barron's, Bloomberg Personal, Forbes, Individual Investor, Money, Mutual Funds, Smart Money, The New York Times,* and *The Wall Street Journal.* Some of the most important information came from scholarly reports in *The Journal of Portfolio Management, The Journal of Finance,* and *Financial Analysts Journal.*

LOST, AND FOUND

After more than a year of concentrated study, I could no longer believe in the Great Predictors. There was simply too much evidence to the contrary. Fortunately, the belief I lost was replaced by a belief in *index funds*—funds that *predictably* track the index they represent because they include all (or a valid sample) of the securities in the index.

While writing this book, I was very much aware that learning about index funds is not an end in itself. Readers want to use their new-found knowledge to *make more money, more reliably.* This ties in with another belief I've acquired: The best investment tool for the great majority of investors is a fully diversified portfolio of index funds (or mostly index funds), balanced to fit investors' individual needs.

In gathering data, I sought and received help from CDA/Wiesenberger, Daniels & Alldredge Investment Management, Ibbotson Associates, Lipper Analytical Services, Morningstar, The Vanguard Group, and other sources of investment information.

I realize this book deflates the basic premise of a mutlitrillion-dollar industry. It is sure to be attacked by mutual fund companies, stock brokerage firms, newsletters, and others. They can attack all they want. They will still have to come up against the hard evidence presented here. When you've seen it, you can make up your own mind.

You may notice many references to The Vanguard Group, a large family of mutual funds. In terms of public index funds, Vanguard has the oldest, largest, and most familiar—the "Index 500 Portfolio," which tracks the Standard & Poor's Index of 500 stocks. Vanguard also has the broadest choice—at least twenty-three index funds, each representing a different type of stock, bond, or money market index. As you might expect, I am a Vanguard customer.

This book is divided into two parts. The first compares index funds with non-index funds and introduces the idea of the optimal portfolio. The second explains how to set up and monitor a superior investment program to fit your needs.

CHAPTER 2

The Emperor
Has No Clothes

ON WATER STREET NEAR THE TIP OF LOWER MANHATTAN, A man sits at his desk on the thirty-second floor of a gleaming office tower. It's dark out. Looking north, a visitor sees a checkerboard of light revealing the financial center of the world.

The office is dimly lit, but the visitor can make out a free-form sculpture in one corner, offset in another by a covey of floor-to-ceiling plants. Abstract oils grace the walls. The chalky glow of a computer monitor lights the man's face as he talks on the phone and stares, frowning, at numbers on the screen. He's telling his wife in their $2 million Montclair, New Jersey, home that he'll be home late, as usual. His clothes display his status: A $2,500 Armani suit; a custom-made, $225 shirt (light blue, with a white collar) from his favorite shop in Hong Kong; paisley-patterned, $125 braces; and $500 shoes (black, of course) from Church of London.

He manages a mutual fund. A sales brochure says his fund has grown by an average of 21 percent a year for the last five years. A stylish graph suggests this was good enough to beat Standard & Poor's Composite Index of 500 Stocks (S&P 500) by a wide margin. He is quoted in *Barron's* and *The Wall Street Journal* and mentioned in *Money*. He has appeared twice on Rukeyser's *Wall Street Week*. For his astute advice, his firm charges investors 1.5 percent of assets per year. Last year he earned $545,000.

What's wrong with this picture?

Strange question. The manager's investors have done well, and he has beaten a universally accepted measure of the stock markets. The fund shareholders are delighted when they see him quoted in business publications. They pride themselves on having entrusted their money to a brilliant, hard-working manager. As for his high income, who could deny he has earned it?

I think you will. Objective evidence will show you why this manager's performance is not what it seems. In fact, you'll learn why he has not earned a nickel's worth of his fee. The same can be said for most of the thousands of alleged wizards who manage $6 trillion in more than 8,000 separate stock or bond mutual funds. The numbers are new; the point is not.

THE $6 TRILLION QUESTION

Way back in 1975, in the summer issue of *The Financial Analysts Journal*, Charles Ellis, founder of Greenwich Research Associates, stated:

> The investment management business is built upon a simple and basic premise: professional managers can beat the market. That premise appears to be false. The ultimate outcome (of the game) is determined by who can lose the fewest points, not who can win the most. Money

mangement has been transformed from a Winner's Game to a Loser's Game.

Mr. Ellis was referring to the fact that the average manager trails his or her relevant index by a significant margin. And there's no reliable way to pick out, *in advance,* which managers will rise above the average. Yet all managers charge substantial fees. Which leads to a logical question about the money invested in non-index mutual funds:

Why pay a premium for inferior performance? That's the $6 trillion question.

A look at the record shows why it's a good question. For the fifteen-year period ending June 30, 1999, a Standard & Poor's (S&P) *index* fund beat 93 percent of diversified stock funds. And this is not a one-time event. The Vanguard Index 500 Portfolio, the largest stock index fund, has outpaced the pack over a wide range of time periods:

VANGUARD INDEX 500 FUND	PERCENT OF NON-INDEX FUNDS OUTPERFORMED
1 year	79
3 years	93
5 years	94
10 years	88
15 years	93
20 years	82

Results as of June 30, 1999.

Source: The Vanguard Group.

Good as it is, this record actually *understates* the power of indexing. The superior performance stated here is based on using *gross* returns—the figures you see published in magazines and sales brochures. I call these figures "gross" because they don't reflect sales charges and other factors that reduce the apparent return of conventional funds. As you'll see in chapter 5, indexing wins even on a gross basis in many different asset classes, from large capitalization stocks to real estate investment trusts. When *net* figures are used, indexing leaves conventional funds even farther behind. More on that to come.

BASIC IDEAS

As you go through this book, you'll notice certain terms and ideas come up again and again. Might as well learn what they mean.

Index

Roughly, a group of stocks or bonds representing a specified portion of the stock or bond markets. Instead of someone's selection, an index includes *all* the securities that meet certain objective criteria, such as market price, country of origin, and type of industry. The Dow Jones Industrial Average—the one you see quoted all the time—is an index that measures the average price of stocks representing thirty massive U.S. companies. The Standard and Poor's Index of 500 Stocks reflects the stock price of more than 500 mostly large companies. When measuring the performance of a conventional fund, you need to compare it with a "relevant" index—one that's in the same asset class as the fund.

Index fund

A mutual fund containing either all or a statistically valid sample of the stocks or bonds in a specified index. The dollar value of each security in the fund is usually proportional to its market capitalization (price times number of securities outstanding). An index *fund* does not exactly match its index, because it has operating expenses that must be deducted from the total return. Also, there may be "tracking error," a slight difference between the fund and the index, caused by technical factors. You can invest in an index fund, but not in an index. In the Introduction, my co-author Burton G. Malkiel explained what makes indexing such a powerful way to invest. In simple terms, it's as though you said to yourself:

> I've got to be realistic. There's no way I can pick out which handful of mutual funds may outperform their relevant index. And based on the record, I don't think anybody else can, either. So what I'll do is buy *all* the stocks or bonds in several asset classes—in other words, index funds. I'll earn more, because index funds have proved they can outperform the average non-index fund. And I'll sleep better, because my return will always nearly match the index return, rain or shine.

Asset class

A group of stocks, bonds, or other kinds of assets with similar characteristics, such as size, price range, growth rate, and industry. Important asset classes include large U.S. corporations (like those in the S&P 500) and large foreign companies in developed countries. In this book, asset classes are divided into "major" asset classes (stocks, bonds, cash) and "subasset" classes—specific *kinds* of stocks and bonds. Asset classes can be represented by indexes, many of which have a corresponding index *fund*. Loosely, you can think of "asset class" and "index" as different ways of saying the same thing.

Index versus non-index

Many investment professionals call conventional funds "actively managed" and refer to index funds as "passively managed." I'm not going to do that. "Passive" implies something negative—people sitting on their hands. On the contrary, index funds require expert management to minimize costs and make sure they stay close to the indexes they represent. Since both types of funds require active management, I call the conventional funds "non-index" funds.

ONWARD AND UPWARD

Index funds held by individual investors have been growing at a remarkable clip. There are now more than 150 publicly available index funds. Rex Sinequefield, Chairman of Dimensional Fund Advisors, summed up the situation as follows:

> Indexing has grown . . . from essentially nothing in 1973 to well over $1 trillion now, and indexing has invaded nearly every asset class. . . . [*Pensions & Investments,* 9/30/96]

Some of these gains can be attributed to publicity in financial and business publications, even though the coverage is often less than it should be. These publications depend on advertisers advertising non-index funds and brokerage operations. You can't expect them to go to the wall for index funds. But there are exceptions. One was the August 1995 issue of *Money.* The Executive Editor's page proclaims:

> Bogle wins: Index funds should be the core of most portfolios today.

("Bogle" refers to John Bogle, chairman of The Vanguard Group.) The headline for the cover story states: "The New Way to Make More Money in Funds." This article was an act of courage and integrity. *Money,* take a bow.

A LETTER THAT
WAS NEVER SENT

There are no guarantees in the stock and corporate bond markets; almost anything can happen. But the inherent advantages of index funds put the wind at your back. We're going to spend the rest of part one of this book establishing the truth of that statement. In the meantime, here's a way to think about the difference between index funds and non-index funds:

> Dear Investor:
>
> We are pleased to inform you that the Ajax Fund grew by 20 percent over the past twelve months. We are proud of this achievement.
>
> However, the fund did not outperform its relevant index, the S&P 500. Funds based on this index grew by 23 percent during the same time period. This means, of course, that you would have earned higher gains in one of the S&P 500 index funds. (Fortunately, Ajax is a no-load fund, or you would have fared even worse.)
>
> Since the only purpose of an actively managed fund is to outperform a relevant index fund, we enclose our check for $11,372 to compensate you for the following items:
>
> - $1,400 to cover our higher administrative, management, and transaction costs. (Index funds commonly operate at one-seventh to one-tenth of the cost of actively managed funds.)
> - $8,432 to cover the difference between what you earned in our fund and what you would have earned in an S&P 500 index fund.
> - $1,540 to cover the extra taxes you will have to pay because the Ajax fund made hundreds of transactions

last year, thus generating capital gains distributions, which, in an index fund, would have been deferred.

We sincerely hope that you choose to leave your money in the Ajax Fund, in the hope of better relative performance during the next twelve months. At the same time, we are obliged to report that the Ajax Fund— along with thousands of other large company growth funds—has failed to outperform an S&P 500 index fund over the most recent ten-year period.

We are most grateful for your confidence in the Ajax Fund and wish you the best of luck in the years ahead.

> Sincerely,
> J. Winthrop Ajax
> President

THE RIGHT PROMISE

This bit of fantasy makes a valid point. You give a fund family a good part of your life savings, and they charge you an average of 1.5 percent (plus .5 percent for transaction fees) to invest your money—assuming there's no sales charge. What you get in return is a service. The fund managers, using their vast resources and legendary skills, promise to try to make your money grow as much as possible, consistent with the fund's rules and objectives.

Now here's the problem: *That's the wrong promise.* What the fund managers should promise is that they will try to beat a specified, relevant index fund. As stated in the letter:

> The only purpose of *non*-index funds is to outperform relevant index funds.

Because if they don't, who needs them? Who needs to go through all the work (and anxiety) of trying to select a non-index fund that will do well *in the future?* Why pay operating expenses that are seven to ten times those of an index fund? Why pay extra capital gains taxes because your fund made so many buy/sell transactions? *The existence of a broad variety of index funds changes the investor's basic perspective.* Now, when you're choosing a mutual fund, you shouldn't ask, "Will this fund make money for me?" You shouldn't even ask, "Will it do better than similar funds?" The right question is, *"Will this fund outperform a relevant index fund?"*

There's another basic change wrought by index *funds* (as opposed to indexes). They provide an objective benchmark that is also a practical investment vehicle. It's like the idea of par in golf. It provides an exact, numerical goal representing what a good player *should* achieve. Not everybody agrees with using indexes—or index funds—as a benchmark. Michael Lipper, president of Lipper Analytical Services, the New York City fund research company, was quoted in *Money* as saying, "It makes much more sense to compare funds to other funds that have a similar investment style and offer the same services."

I do not lightly disagree with a person of his stature, but I do disagree. The two methods of comparing are not mutually exclusive. You can do both, which is exactly the way golf scores are counted—the number of strokes a player has taken, *and* the number of strokes above or below par for the course. Golfers adopted this approach to deal with the possibility that *all* the players turn in a lousy score. In that case, comparing one with another would give you an incomplete picture, which a comparison with par would correct. It's the same with mutual funds—all well and good to compare a fund with its peers, but unless you also compare it with a relevant index fund, you're missing a vital fact.

SLEEP BETTER

Anything can happen to an individual company. You could not only lose, but lose big. If you decide that's not for you, and turn to non-index mutual funds, you've still got problems. There are more than 8,000 separate mutual funds out there. How do you know which ones will suit your needs and beat the average? The quick answer is, "You don't." You'll see why as we move along.

Contrast that with index funds, where you deal with a relatively small number of important asset classes (such as big-company stocks, real estate stocks, long-term bonds). Yes, they fluctuate in market value. But here's the point:

> With index funds, you *know* your money will always equal its relevant index (minus low operating expenses and a small tracking error)—*guaranteed.*

This is inherently more comforting than having to worry about your non-index funds underperforming their relevant index. Also, index funds relieve you of the burden of trying to time the market. By their nature, index funds are long-term investments, not appropriate for trading in and out. Index funds give you less to think about, less to worry about, less to do. Which brings up a useful idea.

DEMOCRACY COMES TO INVESTING

Index funds *simplify* investing. You don't have to confront the forbidding task of choosing from thousands of stocks and bonds or thousands of mutual funds. You don't have to belong to that elite club known as "active investors," trying to find needles in a haystack. Equally important, you don't have to hire somebody else to do it for you. That's good, because the average professional has rarely matched the long-term performance of a relevant index fund, yet charges a significant fee. The wall of mystique that Wall Street has erected in front of you is no longer an obstacle. You just walk around it. Index funds have brought democracy to investing.

A NEW WAY OF THINKING

Wall Street has been afraid to recognize the obvious: Index funds have ushered in a new approach to investing, a new paradigm. To make that clear, let's look at a quick sketch of the history of investing. I've divided it into five basic approaches:

1. Buy individual stocks and bonds from brokerage firms (from the 1890s)

Stock brokerage firms peddled securities directly to individual investors, many of whom hoped to make a killing in the market. The panic of 1929–1930 showed that the killing could cut both ways. In the fifties and sixties, brokerage firms hired security analysts to bring professional discipline to the analysis of stocks and bonds. Paradoxically, this did not necessarily make the firms' recommendations more useful. Competing security analysts made the markets more sensitive and competitive, which tended to offset the potential benefits of improved analysis.

2. Supplement stocks and bonds with mutual funds offered by salespeople (from the 1950s)

Mutual funds were a great leap forward. They enabled individual investors of modest means to diversify their investments and get professional management. That was important, because diversification lowers risk. Mutual funds also brought a useful simplicity to the process of investing. It became easy to invest every month, and monthly statements recorded your progress.

3. Buy no-load mutual funds directly from a mutual fund company (from the 1970s)

Gradually, some mutual fund companies began offering to invest people's money directly, dispensing with the need for a salesperson—and a sales commission. Some people argued that load funds must be better because they charge more. But they weren't (and aren't). Nearly all the sales commission goes to the salesperson or into advertising the funds. The "load" contributes little or nothing to hiring better managers, building better software, or doing better research.

4. Buy mutual funds where you work through a tax-deferred savings plan (from the late 1970s)

In 1978 Congress passed a law allowing individuals to accumulate savings and investments on a tax-deferred basis, provided they were enrolled in a "defined contribution plan." For employees of profit-making companies, the plan is called a 401(k) (referring to a section of the law). For nonprofit employees, it's a 403(b). And for government workers, it's a 457. In some organizations, employers add to the employee's contribution to enhance loyalty. Defined contribution plans have become a major form of individual investing. ("Defined contribution" means the amount you contribute is specified; what you take out is not.) You may not think of yourself as an investor, but if you're in a defined contribution plan, you may have many thousands of dollars invested in the stock and bond markets.

5. Buy no-load **index** mutual funds instead of individual securities or non-index funds (mainly from the early 1990s)

This is the new paradigm for investing by individuals. Index funds have been around since the early 1970s, when professional investors started using them for pension programs. One of the first champions of indexing was my co-author, Burton G. Malkiel. In his best-selling book, *A Random Walk Down Wall Street*, he states:

> What we need is a no-load, minimum-management-fee mutual fund that simply buys the hundreds of stocks making up the broad stock market averages and does no trading from security to security in an attempt to catch the winners. Whenever below-average performance on the part of any mutual fund is noticed, fund spokesmen are quick to point out, "You can't buy the averages." It's time the public could.

Quite independently, John Bogle, Chairman of The Vanguard Group, came to the same conclusion. He started an S&P 500 index fund for individual investors in 1976. It often beat the average performance of diversified stock funds, but not many people took notice until the mid-nineties, when the fund *doubled* in market value. Critics like to say that indexing is "settling for mediocrity." "Go for a home run," they urge. So much for that argument.

The recent success of this and other index funds has led the business press to give index funds more attention. Today you can use index funds to invest in a wide range of stock and bond asset classes—from the huge stocks in the Dow all the way down to funds that mirror the Russell 2,000 index of small capitalization stocks.

Another important development in the nineties was the birth of the mutual fund supermarket, a central source from which you can buy any of thousands of mutual funds and be treated like a single customer. Charles Schwab & Co. launched the first one in 1992. They soon had major competition from Fidelity, Jack White, and others.

WHAT ABOUT INDIVIDUAL
STOCKS AND BONDS?

You don't need them. For the average person, mutual funds are a better alternative—especially index mutual funds. Think of the problems with individual stocks and bonds:

- Most people can't afford to buy cost-efficient amounts of enough different stocks for adequate diversification. If you try to get around this problem by buying a little of this and a little of that, the commissions can kill you.
- You have to make at least four hard decisions: Which securities to buy, which to sell, when to buy, and when to sell. It would be a mistake to minimize the difficulty of any of these decisions. There is a common notion that you're home free when you buy a stock that goes up. Not so. *You don't pocket a gain until you sell the security.* Knowing the best time to do that is something most people are not equipped to determine. Keep in mind, also, that you have to make all those decisions for every stock or bond you own. With index funds, you don't have to choose securities, and you don't have to time the markets.
- In making those four decisions, you compete with highly informed professionals who have access to data and software that mere mortals like you and I can't even imagine. In the vast majority of cases, by the time you and I actually buy or sell a security, the news we acted on is already reflected in the price.
- You pay high commissions to buy and sell individual stocks and bonds. At a big discount broker, the cost of buying or selling $10,000 worth of stock is $110. That's 1.1 percent when you buy, and 1.1 percent when you sell. A total of 2.2 percent. (The commission rate on small amounts may be even higher.) Compare that with investing in a no-load S&P 500 index

fund, where the cost can be less than one-fifth of one percent a year, 25 percent of which is deducted from dividend income every quarter. In the fund, you start out with the entire $10,000 working for you. At the broker, you start out with $9,890.

- It's hard to manage individual stocks and bonds. It takes a lot of time, effort, and knowledge to stay on top of a portfolio, and at tax time, it can be a horror. Fund families, on the other hand, give you a single statement that reflects your total situation, including the percent of your money in stocks, bonds, and cash, plus the amount of your total return that is currently taxable.

- We live in a period of accelerating change. More and more, as time goes on, if you're going to buy or sell a stock, you have to do it *fast*. The average person—even the average active investor—is simply not equipped to respond to kaleidoscopic markets.

- Brokerage firms are glad to offer recommendations about which stocks and bonds to buy. In effect, you pay commissions to trade, but get the advice free. This is less wonderful than it may seem. Every recommendation is essentially a prediction of future events. The last time I checked, human beings were somewhat deficient in that area. Think about it. If broker recommendations were the road to riches, a lot more people would be rich. The same applies to the predictions by people who write for publications and newsletters.

- Studies have shown that up to 92 percent of the variation in return on a diversified portfolio can come not from picking hot stocks, but from "asset allocation." This is a major concept we'll discuss later. For now, know that asset allocation refers primarily to the percentage of stocks, bonds, and cash in your portfolio. The term also refers to the *types* of securities you hold within the broad categories of stocks, bonds, and cash.

A FEW SAMPLES OF
WHAT YOU'LL LEARN

As mentioned, this book is divided into two parts. The first part documents the fact that index funds are almost always a better way to invest than conventional mutual funds, especially on an after-tax basis. The second part, "The Five Giant Steps to Wealth," explains how you can use what you've learned to make more money. Here are some of the subjects we'll cover:

- Why index funds are likely to continue outperforming the average non-index fund
- How index funds simplify investing
- Why index funds provide more *reliable* investment results
- Why over 90 percent of your investment return may come from a single investment decision
- The crucial importance of financial and investment planning
- How to combine different kinds of index funds to maximize return and minimize risk
- How to choose which funds to put in your portfolio

BEGINNERS OR EXPERTS

You can profit from this book even if you don't know much about investing and don't think of yourself as an investor. I will show you how index funds can give you higher returns than the average non-index fund, along with more peace of mind. On the other hand, if you're an active, informed investor, you'll learn how you could become more successful than ever before. In fact:

If you think of all the professional money managers as "Wall Street," the odds are that index funds will enable you to "beat the Street," which means you're likely to get better returns than most fund managers, even before adjusting for sales charges, risk, and taxes.

But what about the hypothetical Great Predictor we met at the start of this chapter? Surely you couldn't have done better than his scorching, five-year gain of 21 percent a year? Yes, you could. He runs what's called a "Small Cap Value Fund." His relevant index is the "Value" portion of the Russell 2,000 index, which grew by 23 percent during the same time period. If you were in a Russell 2,000 Value index fund, you would have beaten him. No problem.

WHY INDEX FUNDS ARE
JUST CATCHING ON

Despite recent fast growth and good press, the money invested in index funds is still just a splash compared with the ocean of money in non-index funds. How can that be? If index funds are all that good, why aren't they a bigger part of the investment picture? Four answers come to mind:

1. Human nature

People want to believe in Santa Claus—even smart, sophisticated people. They want to believe there are gifted gurus who can reliably outperform the markets.

2. Publicity about non-index fund performance

You can't help reading and hearing about funds that have beaten the markets by a wide margin. The noise level is deafening. You see headlines like, "SuperTech Fund gains a sizzling 43 percent in first half." You'd have to be less than human not to be affected by all the trumpets and drum beats.

3. Greed and fear

For mutual fund companies and brokerage firms, no-load index funds are a lot less profitable than non-index funds. Investors typically pay five to seven times more for a so-called actively managed fund than for an index fund. The sobering truth is, there's a big, powerful industry out there that depends on investors not fully appreciating the advantages of indexing. Indexing threatens a lot of mortgage payments in places like Fairfield County, Connecticut, and Orange County, California. The people who pay those mortgages are not likely to run around promoting investments that could drive them out of their castles.

4. Just plain ignorance

Most people don't know much about index funds. A common response when I tell people about this book is, "What's an index fund?" They've heard about them, but they're not familiar with them. They don't know the record of index funds versus conventional funds. They don't know you can buy index funds in a wide range of asset classes.

WHY BOTHER?

Skim through this book, and you'll see that it covers a lot of ground. Your response could be one or both of the following:

> Look. I appreciate what you're trying to do, but I just don't have the time. I'm putting in sixty hours a week on the job, and when I get home, investing is not exactly on the top of my list.

> I know I should read this book, but I'm just not that interested in investing. To tell you the truth, it bores me. I know that's not smart, but that's how I feel.

Fair enough. But give me a minute, if you would. Acting on those sentiments, you're likely to do whatever's easiest. Maybe you just delegate the whole thing to a friend or relative who's in the business and forget about it. Why not do that? For a couple of reasons:

One is that we're talking about your life savings, whether they're currently thousands or millions. And it's not just the money. It's what kind of college your kids will go to. It's what kind of home you'll live in. It's how well you can retire.

Another reason is the issue of what your friend or relative will actually do. He or she will probably handle your money according to generally accepted practices, such as:

- Investing all your money in stocks and bonds or in non-index funds
- Selecting funds largely on the basis of their published track records
- Trying to time the markets by trading (buying and selling) the different funds you own
- Earning his or her income by charging a commission on the trades
- Trying to diversify by buying different funds or stocks and bonds in the same asset class

All these generally accepted practices have one thing in common: *They are all wrong.* They are against your best interests. Your Uncle Charley may do well by following these practices, especially during roaring bull markets. But however well he does, the odds are that you will do even better by using the approach this book recommends.

SUMMARY

- Stock index funds in a variety of asset classes have outperformed the average, diversified non-index fund over many different time periods. Bond index funds have a similar record.

- The only purpose of non-index funds is to beat a relevant index fund. Managers who fail to do that don't earn their compensation.
- Non-index fund performance may not be as good as it seems. For one thing, it has to be measured against a relevant index. In addition, you need to consider the effect of taxes, sales charges, expenses, and the amount of risk taken to achieve the return.
- Index funds are the new paradigm for individual and institutional investors.
- Index funds simplify investing. Instead of having to choose from among thousands of securities or thousands of mutual funds, you can choose from a small number of important asset classes.
- People don't need individual stocks or bonds, which generate avoidable costs and other problems. For the vast majority of people, index funds are a better alternative.
- When judging a non-index fund, it's vital to compare its record not only with similar funds, but also with a relevant index.

Welcome to the new world of investing. Things will never be the same.

CHAPTER 3

Smoke, Mirrors, and Crystal Balls

If index funds are so good, how come I see such high return figures for non-index funds?"

Fair question. One answer is that some funds do beat their relevant indexes in some years. The only trouble is, you can't tell which ones will do it next year. A second answer has more to do with the world that Alice found in *Through the Looking Glass:*

> *"When I use a word," Humpty Dumpty said, in a rather scornful tone, "it means just what I choose it to mean—neither more nor less."*

Substitute *number* for *word*, and you get the general idea. If Alice were to look at the reported returns of non-index funds, she would find much to wonder at. Ads in one issue of a personal finance magazine, for example, had the following headlines:

"77.49 %"

"America's #1 Growth Fund."

"#1 Performing Fund Since the Market Low of 1987."

Wait a minute. If I want to put my money in the fund with the hottest track record, which do I choose? Which is the real Number One? The Vanguard funds newsletter *In the Vanguard* explains what's going on:

For promotional purposes, mutual fund sponsors have the ability [are permitted by the SEC] to choose any time period for performance measurement. Sponsors are also permitted to limit the field of competitive funds by asset size. As a result, a fund could lay claim to the top spot by comparing itself to, say, similar funds with less than $250 million in assets. Since funds may define the group, asset size, and time period, literally hundreds of funds can lay claim to #1 stature at any one time.

This is a useful insight. It means that when you see non-index funds boasting about their rank, you have to know what universe they're talking about. The universe used for the ad could be so small that the return figures, although true, lose much of their meaning. It's like saying, "I'm the fastest woman alive—in this house."

If Alice were to continue her study of non-index returns, she would find that things get "curiouser and curiouser." More specifically, I think she would conclude that reported returns should not—must not—be taken at face value. In fact, there are at least eight points to keep in mind when you evaluate the returns of non-index funds:

1. WHAT YOU GET MAY NOT BE WHAT YOU KEEP

When an uninformed person sees a glittering return published by a non-index fund, she or he may be inclined to think, "Look how much I could have earned!" Not necessarily. It depends in part on the fund's turnover and the person's tax bracket. Here's the story:

As mentioned, an index fund rarely trades a security. It buys only when a stock or bond not in the index qualifies for membership; it sells only when a security no longer meets the index's specifications or when the company is merged out of existence. The result is very low *turnover* (the frequency of trades). Compare, for example, the turnover rates of ten large mutual funds, ranked by their size in 1996.

FUND	TURNOVER
Vanguard Index 500	4%
American: Investment Co. of America	21
American: Washington Mutual	23
American: Income Fund of America	26
Vanguard Windsor	32
Fidelity Growth & Income	67
Fidelity Puritan	76
20th Century Ultra	87
Fidelity Magellan	155
Fidelity Contrafund	223

If we take the twenty largest funds, instead of just the top ten, the average turnover of this group climbs to 97 percent, which means the average fund traded nearly its entire portfolio in the preceding 12-month period (Sources: *The New York Times*, September 15, 1996, and Morningstar, Inc., the Chicago fund research company). In contrast, turnover for Vanguard's Index 500 was only 4 percent.

Low turnover is good. Instead of piling up taxable capital gains in bull markets, you can defer your taxes until you take the money out of the fund. Eventually, you may have to pay capital gains taxes on any amount you withdraw from the fund. But at that point, you (or your spouse or children) may be in a lower tax bracket than when the gains were earned. More important, all the money that would otherwise have gone to taxes has been working for you. Over time, that can make a big difference in the size of your nest egg—even with a lower tax on long-term capital gains.

How much these taxes hurt your return depends on your tax status. If all your investments are in a 401(k) or similar tax-deferred plan, this problem won't affect you. Your capital gains taxes are automatically deferred (although you may have to pay taxes when you make withdrawals).

But if you have taxable current investments—and especially if you're in a high or medium tax bracket—a high turnover can devour a big slice of your after-tax return. Nowhere is this issue more thoroughly explored than in a paper by economists Joel M. Dixon and John B. Shoven (*Center for Economic Policy Research*, Stanford University, April 1993). They examined pretax and posttax returns for a sample of sixty-two mutual funds over a thirty-year period, running from 1963 through 1992. Among their findings:

- Investors in high tax brackets pocketed only 45 percent of the returns published by mutual funds.
- Before taxes, $10,000 invested in 1963 would have grown to $218,900 over the ten-year period; after taxes, a high-income investor would have only $98,700.
- Changes in fund rankings (pretax to after-tax) were substantial even for investors in intermediate tax brackets.
- For the high-tax investor, Vanguard's Index 500 fund would have outperformed 92 percent of the funds in the study, if all realized capital gains could have been deferred (ten-year period ending 12/31/92).

Dixon and Shoven come to this conclusion:

> Our calculations show that the relative rankings of funds
> on a post-tax basis . . . differ dramatically from the pub-
> lished pre-tax rankings. That is, taxable investors cannot
> easily and reliably determine which of two funds would
> have offered them a better after-tax return with the pub-
> licly available information.

The authors would like to see mutual funds offer post-tax information in advertising and prospectuses. So would I. Large
mutual fund families have addressed the tax issue by offering
"tax-managed" index funds in which nearly all capital gains are
deferred.

Conclusion: If you're investing in a taxable account, don't buy
a fund just because it has a record of high returns. Check into its
turnover history (and sales charge). As a rule of thumb, the larger
the turnover, the worse you'll do after taxes. Ask your accountant
to estimate what your *net* returns would have been during the return period. Then compare that number with the net return of a
relevant index fund over the same period. Keep in mind that none
of this discussion applies to tax-deferred accounts, such as a 401(k).

2. WHAT YOU DON'T
SEE CAN HURT YOU

A table in the September 15, 1996, edition of *The New York Times*
reveals that ten of the twenty largest non-index mutual funds
had sales charges ranging from 3 percent to 5.75 percent. Notice
that when you see mutual fund performance figures, they do *not*
include sales charges. If you put $10,000 into a fund with a 5.75
percent sales load, you start with $9,475, not $10,000. Over time,
the missing $575 can make a significant difference in the money
you earn.

Example: Say you invest $10,000 in a non-index fund with a typical cost structure—a 5.75 percent sales charge and operating costs of 1.5 percent. It performs well, returning an average of 10 percent (compounded monthly) for twenty years, which would bring you $73,281. Except for three things:

- The sales charge itself.
- The annual operating costs.
- The loss caused by not having this money growing for you. Together, these costs add up to $22,533, reducing your net return to $50,748, instead of $73,281. Your annual total return drops from 10 percent to 8.15 percent (figures adapted from *Index Mutual Funds,* W. Scott Simon, Namborn Publishing, 1998).

Your salesperson may tell you that's a small price to pay for good performance. Wrong. The available evidence says that "load" funds (those with a sales charge) perform no better than "no-load" funds (no sales charge). In the table mentioned above, *The New York Times* reports:

Who says you get what you pay for? Of the 20 largest stock funds, half charge you to get in. But the best performers tend to be those that don't charge. Seven of the 20 funds have had double-digit returns in 1996; of those, 5 are no-load funds. That group includes the best performer among the largest funds this year, the Janus fund. The worst performer in 1996 is also the largest and one that charges a fee. . . .

Of course, that's only for one year. In his best-selling *Guide to Successful No-Load Fund Investing,* author Sheldon Jacobs cites four different studies from 1962 to 1994. Each comes to the same conclusion: *No-load funds perform just as well as, or better than, load funds.* We'll take a closer look at investment costs, including hidden "12b-1" fees, in a later chapter.

The May 11, 1997, issue of *The New York Times* showed that a dozen funds with more than $100 million in assets and charging a management fee of at least one percent were in the *bottom 10 percent* of their categories over the three-year period ended February 28, 1997. Keep in mind that the management fee is only part of the total expense figure.

Conclusion: As a rule, it pays to avoid funds with sales charges in any form. There is no objective reason to believe they will do any better than pure no-loads. Fortunately, most index funds are pure no-loads.

3. WHAT YOU SEE
MAY BE JUST LUCK

Like *manager risk, luck* is a term that is seldom used on Wall Street. Of course not. There are six-figure bonuses at stake. Even the idea of luck is a threat. Nevertheless, we're going to consider the possibility of luck. To do that, we need to understand the difference between two statements:

"A" is *caused* by "B."
"A" is *associated with* "B."

Many people, including investors, routinely get these two statements mixed up. Suppose I were to show you that the amount of rainfall in Chicago closely tracks the level of short-term interest rates. Or that full moons are associated with the average number of pigeons on a statue in Cedar Rapids. You'd probably say these events are just coincidences. They occur together, but one does not *cause* the other. But how about this association:

Every year, some fund managers earn more than the return on their relevant index. That proves these managers have superior skills.

A huge, powerful industry would have you accept this statement as gospel. It's not. Fund managers are no more exempt from the laws of chance than rainfall in Chicago or pigeons in Cedar Rapids. The fact is, fund managers who outperformed their relevant index may simply have been lucky. You can see that on a common-sense basis: Even if you take published returns at face value, only a handful of managers have ever been able to sustain a winning streak long term. The number drops to minuscule proportions when you account for taxes and sales charges.

The essential point to understand is that the parameters of chance can be surprisingly wide. John Bogle makes this point with a graph showing the results of one hundred people flipping a coin ten times. The most frequent ratio of heads to tails is, as you would expect, five heads and five tails. But a few coin flippers get nine heads and one tail (or nine tails and one head)—far from the average. He then compares the results of coin flipping with the returns of the one hundred largest growth and value mutual funds over a ten-year period. The pattern of returns is strikingly similar to the results of coin flipping. (Bogle points out that the comparison should not be taken literally—the mathematics of coin flipping is different from that of mutual fund returns.) But the main point remains: Deviations from the average do not necessarily imply superior skill. Bogle ends the comparison with this delicious sentence:

A winning coin flipper commands no press interest; a winning fund manager is acclaimed a near genius.

4. WHAT YOU SEE MAY BE HIGH-COST INDEXING

Imagine that you and I meet for lunch to talk about your investments. When the coffee is served, I pose a question: "Why don't you and I start a mutual fund?" "We have no credentials," you say. No problem. It's time to introduce you to the wonders of "closet indexing." This is a term the industry uses to refer to money managers who buy the stocks in one or more indexes. They pretend to be active managers—and probably buy a few stocks on judgment—but mainly they index. There's no quantitative data on how much of this goes on, but it does go on. Nothing to stop us from doing the same thing.

First step (after we get start-up money) is to invent a plausible investment style. It might be, for example, "undervalued growth stocks with low dividend yield." We tell people that we have a software model that sorts out those stocks for us. Then we cook up a nonexistent system to time our purchases and sales, being careful to note that our main timing strategy is to buy and hold, which reduces portfolio turnover.

The rest is detail. We hire an ad agency and a public relations firm to do our marketing. And—you'll like this part—we don't even have to buy and sell stocks. All we do is buy a sensible mix of index funds from a low-cost producer, paying .2 percent or .3 percent in operating costs. Then we retail the funds at 1.5 percent, which is about average for non-index funds. This gives us a four- to six-time mark-up on our product. We don't even need a sales charge. Acapulco here we come.

What will happen? A steady stream of articles and ads in the right publications will bring in money, which we use to buy index funds. And since we have a mix of asset classes, our fund will seem to do well, despite the unconscionable fee for what we're doing. Stay with this for a few years, and I won't have to write books about investing, and you won't have to read them.

5. WHAT YOU SEE MAY
NOT BE WHAT YOU GET

Suppose you decide your portfolio needs a certain kind of small-company fund. Being a logical person, you approach a fund that advertises itself as that kind of fund. Will you get what you're looking for? Not necessarily. The fund may not be what it says it is.

Welcome to the wonderland of *style drift*. This term refers to what happens when non-index fund managers buy stocks or bonds that do not reflect their announced management approach. They do this because the Great Predictors are under enormous pressure to perform. If they think they can't get enough performance from the kinds of stocks or bonds they're supposed to buy, many of them buy other kinds. The result is "cap creep." Example: During the late nineties, many small-cap managers bought larger stocks to try to get in on the popularity of large-cap stocks.

Cap creep goes down, as well as up. When large-cap stocks don't seem to be doing well, a large-cap manager may start buying midcap or even small-cap stocks in hopes of getting a faster ride. Once again, investors are left in the dark. The Securities and Exchange Commission is in the process of clamping down on funds that don't deliver what their name and published descriptions imply. But it may be a long time before the results show up in promotional literature.

The discrepancies produced by style drift are more important than you might think, as an article in the October 1995 *Institutional Investor* explains:

> Plan administrators are beginning to grumble, with good reason, about mutual funds that seem to stray from their investment styles. . . . "I've seen small-cap value funds grow into large-cap growth stock funds," says Putnam senior vice president and equity specialist Bruce George. Not surprisingly, plan sponsors . . . were not happy with funds' lack of reliability. Companies don't want the options they offer to 401(k) participants to wander all over the risk-reward spectrum or change styles willy-nilly.

Neither should you. When you buy a fund, you expect it to move your portfolio in a certain direction. If the fund misrepresents itself, that may not happen. Which means your portfolio may not be invested according to plan.

An April 1996 article in *Pension Management* raises another issue: Nobody's good at everything. The article describes why a former star performer among small-cap non-index funds fell from the limelight:

> Management decided to change the capitalization weightings of the fund to keep that performance going and started looking to different sectors where they didn't necessarily have expertise.

Most fund managers specialize in one or, at most, a few asset classes. When they step out of their specialty, they put themselves at a competitive disadvantage—and the investor may be the loser.

Professionals deal with style drift by using expensive software that analyzes a fund's composition by the percentage of different asset classes it holds. But what can civilians like you and I do? Consider index funds. If you want to invest in midcap stocks, for example, buy a fund that closely tracks a midcap index. When you do that, you can be reasonably certain you're getting what you asked for.

Conclusion: Style drift is a significant problem for investors in many non-index funds. Investing in index funds provides a practical solution.

6. WHAT YOU SEE MAY BE
A MISLEADING AVERAGE

Incredible as it may seem, you can lose a lot of money in a fund with a terrific record. It depends on when you come into the game. A relatively small fund may have outstanding gains when it first starts. This attracts a flood of new money. Typically, the fund manager has trouble investing all that money. Buying more of the original stocks may drive up their price, and there just aren't that many great ideas out there. The fund's return plummets. Now here's the tricky part. At the end of the calendar year, the fund can still post an impressive average gain because of its sensational start, thus luring more new money. But the only investors who do well are those who bought at the very beginning and held on. Late buyers lose. An August 1997 issue of *The New York Times* documented this point:

> Last year, for example, the [name of fund] reported a 51 percent gain in its first 11 months of operation while actually losing $31 million of investors' money.

Conclusion: A *fund's* return may be a lot higher than the average *investor's* return. To deal with this problem, look at a wide variety of time periods. Otherwise, you could find yourself investing in obsolete performance.

7. WHAT YOU SEE
MAY NOT BE REAL

What do you buy when you buy shares in a non-index fund? You don't get a piece of a factory. You don't get a tangible product you can touch and feel. What you get is somebody's judgment. At some companies, the somebody is a committee. Usually, though, it's just one person, a single manager whose smiling face, more and more often, appears in advertising. Mutual funds have gone to a star system.

There's nothing wrong with all that. You want a star, you get a star. But what happens when the star leaves the fund? Do you follow the star? Or do you stay with the fund company, since it created the environment and the investment guidelines that helped the star succeed? An article in the October 1996 issue of *Smart Money* discusses this subject. The title, "Mutual Funds Can Rewrite History," gives you an idea of the article's general thrust, which may be described as somewhat less than reverential:

> Thanks to those vigilant watchdogs at the Securities and Exchange Commission, figuring out the performance record of a mutual fund is about to get significantly harder. Unless regulators have a change of heart, you'll soon see managers goosing their returns and funds touting track records from years in which they didn't even exist.

The article explains that the SEC has allowed at least one fund manager to use her record at fund A to sell fund B, where she now presides. Since then, the SEC has imposed strict limitations on the extent to which this sort of thing can go on. But the basic practice is still allowed.

Conclusion: Non-index funds with mixed track records and funds that have lost a star manager are hard to evaluate. Index funds, operating without subjective investment decisions, don't have that problem.

8. WHAT YOU SEE ARE THE ONES LEFT STANDING

So far we've been talking mostly about things to consider when evaluating the performance of *individual* non-index funds. Now we're going to compare *classes* of funds: non-index versus index.

To do that, let's go back to the mutual fund company you and I formed in point 4. A few years have passed, and we're doing well. Of course we are. We're working with a high mark-up in a business with low expenses. But we're getting restless. We want to branch out, get bigger, make more money. So we decide to start more funds. Not being a pair of dummies, we realize that most people buy funds on the basis of past performance. This stops us for awhile, since neither of us has the foggiest idea of how to get good performance. But we do know that some asset classes will go up while others go down. From this comes a scheme: Start a fund in *each* of six or eight asset classes. That way, we're almost sure to have a couple of winners—funds that beat their relevant index (before taxes and sales charges).

"But," you say, "what about the funds that go down?" No problem. We quietly merge them into our original fund, say a few words, and bury their records. We're left with a few winners, which the media will tout for us. The money pours in, because everybody thinks we're brilliant. It can't miss.

I wish I could tell you this is pure fantasy. But it's not. Many fund companies start nonpublic "incubator" funds. They take them public if, and only if, they outperform their asset class. The published growth record, of course, is always impressive. This attracts a flood of money from investors, at which point things can go wrong. A manager suddenly swamped with money may find it hard to maintain the quality of his or her original stock selections. Happens all the time.

For evidence of this cut-and-try approach, let's look at some numbers provided by Lipper Analytical Services.

Year	Number of Mutual Funds
1980	446
1985	830
1990	2,044
1997	8,000+

Does this rocketing growth represent an industry racing to keep up with demand? Or is there something else going on? Here's what *Money* magazine reported in its August 1995 issue:

To sponsors, a fund is a winner if it sells; for you it's a winner only if it excels. "The industry isn't even trying to assume the high moral ground of putting shareholders first," says Don Phillips, president of Morningstar Mutual Funds, the Chicago fund rating service. "It's more like, How do we maintain our robust 25 percent or better profit margin?" Among the practices we found to be potentially harmful to shareholders:

- Companies often crank out new funds mainly to attract assets, not because the products represent great new investment ideas.
- To stand out from funds with similar strategies and goals, some managers load up on risky securities.
- To compensate for the return-sapping effects of high fees, some managers skew the way they run their portfolios—and your money.

The article goes on to quote Stan Egener, president of Neuberger & Berman:

There are people in this industry who put out funds simply because they can be sold. . . . I think more choices means more confusion. No stock analyst covers thousands of stocks, yet we're asking people who don't do this for a living to choose from that many funds—it's mind boggling.

If some companies start funds "simply because they can be sold," then withdraw the losers, how does that affect published returns? Fortunately, we don't have to wonder. An authoritative study by my co-author proves that "survivorship bias" has a significant impact on the relative performance of mutual funds (*Journal of Finance*, June 1995). As mentioned in his introduction, Malkiel found a significant difference between the returns earned by *all* funds and the returns earned by *surviving* funds:

We find that the dollar-weighted average return for all funds, including those that were liquidated during the period, was [significantly] less than the average of surviving funds and substantially below the returns from the S&P index.... The differences are even more dramatic for the 15-year period ending December, 31, 1991. The average return for equity funds surviving over the whole 15-year period was 18.7 percent per annum. The average yearly return for all funds including non-survivors, was only 14.5 percent.

The average return of all *surviving* funds will always be inflated for a simple reason: Fund companies don't kill winners; they kill losers. Darwin comes to Wall Street.

Conclusion: When you see published returns for groups of non-index mutual funds, remember these returns are *overstated* by fund companies eliminating poor-performing funds during the measured period. This problem does not apply to index funds.

EVEN YOUR EMPLOYER

You would think that your employer, being a professional investor through the company's tax-deferred investment plan, would be protected from doctored data. Not so. Even plan sponsors get fuzzy numbers from mutual funds. To its credit, the mutual fund industry has established programs to correct this problem. One of these is the Association for Investment Management and Research (AIMR), which recently set new and more precise standards for giving data to plan sponsors. But according to an article in the April 1, 1996, issue of *Pensions & Investments*, the results have been somewhat less than encouraging:

Consultants and other experts say as many as one-third of the managers claiming to be complying with the [AIMR] standards might not be doing so. . . . And some managers still are cherry-picking their results and including only the best accounts in performance composites, even though the standards were designed to stop that practice. . . . The standards allow for plenty of leeway for money managers to juice up performance reporting to enhance their positions in manager search data bases, according to these sources.

SUMMARY

There are at least eight reasons to question the performance of non-index funds:

1. Taxes on capital gains and dividend income may eat up a large part of your apparent gain

The average diversified stock fund has a turnover of about 85 percent. In a rising market, this generates capital gains—and capital gains taxes. With taxable money, the net return for high-tax investors can be less than half the published return. Medium-tax investors also suffer sizable losses. This point does not apply to tax-deferred accounts, such as a 401(k).

2. Sales charges can significantly lower your return

Running to as much as 6 percent of assets, these charges can significantly reduce an investor's net return, no matter how the charge is levied—up front or over time.

3. Your manager may have just been lucky

With thousands of non-index funds in the running, some are bound to beat the others, just on the basis of luck, which usually doesn't last. That's one reason past performance does not predict future success.

4. Your non-index manager may be a closet indexer

These managers put your money into the same stocks that are in a relevant index, while you pay top dollar for subjective management.

5. Your manager may have changed his or her investment style

When managers can't get enough index-beating performance using their announced investment approach, some of them resort to other approaches, such as style drift. This changes the product the investor bought, and takes the manager into areas where he or she is more likely to make mistakes.

6. The fund's average return may be misleading

An average return, especially over a short time period, may hide a disturbing recent trend.

7. The apparent return on your fund may reflect the record of another fund

At this writing, fund managers who move from one fund to another are allowed to use their previous track record in citing results of their new fund. This makes the new record hard to evaluate and raises a troubling question: Do I follow the manager? Or stay with the fund?

8. The performance of groups of non-index funds is overstated by the withdrawal of funds that failed

Non-index fund companies routinely start a large number of funds as a marketing tool, then withdraw the ones that don't succeed. Result: Non-index returns for any given asset class are significantly overstated, especially in the long term.

CHAPTER 4

What's Performance?

E VALUATING THE RETURN ON *ANY* KIND OF FUND—INDEX OR non-index—is not as simple as it seems. Usually, *return* is short for *average, annual compound rate of total return* (also called *performance*). *Compound* refers to building on a growing base, with capital gains and dividends reinvested. *Total return* means a combination of the components:

1. The gain or loss caused by an asset's change in price during a specified time ("capital gain" or "capital loss")
2. Dividend income from stocks, or interest income from bonds

Dividends are a way of distributing earnings to shareholders. They're a more important source of total return on stocks than many investors realize. Half of the long-term return on the S&P 500, for example, has come from dividends. (In the race for capital gains, this point is often overlooked.) For small stocks, which are usually bought for growth, the percentage of total return from dividends is usually lower, or even nonexistent.

Another term you'll see is *yield*. For stocks, it's the dividend income expressed as a percentage of its current price. The average long-term dividend yield for the S&P 500, for example, is about 4 percent. For bonds, yield is usually short for "yield to maturity," the amount of interest you'll collect if you hold a bond until it matures, expressed as a percentage of the purchase price. Yield includes any capital gains or losses that may have occurred. Example: Say that by the time a $1,000 bond matures, you've collected $60 in interest. We would then say the bond "yielded" 6 percent.

That ought to do it for now. Let's move on.

FOUR FACTS TO CONSIDER WHEN JUDGING RETURNS

As we saw in the previous chapter—and will see again—you can't take non-index fund returns at face value. Here are four facts to remember when you judge the return on *any* kind of mutual fund:

Fact No. 1. *The stock and bond markets consist of diverse asset classes*

As mentioned, an asset class is a group of stocks, bonds, or other kinds of assets with similar characteristics, such as size, price range, growth rate, and industry. Important asset classes include the stocks of large U.S. corporations and short-term obligations of the federal government. There are at least two major reasons to focus on asset classes:

Different asset classes usually carry different degrees of risk—and offer different rates of return. A 10 percent return on risky small-cap growth stocks would be a yawn, while 10 percent on low-risk, long-term bonds would be sensational.

Different asset classes respond differently to the same economic or market events. Owning a variety of asset classes averages out the volatility of a group of securities. While one class is going down, another may be going up.

Emphasizing asset classes runs counter to conventional wisdom. Most investors and popular investment publications focus on individual stocks and bonds and individual mutual funds. Many funds, for example, brag about their "stock picking" ability. This, as we'll see, is far less important than how you choose and allocate asset classes. "Institutional" investors (insurance companies, banks, large employers) know this. They tend to focus on what percentage of money they have in various asset classes. So will we. But first let's get into our subject a little more deeply.

When it comes to financial assets, you can't get more basic than *stocks*, *bonds*, and *cash*. How you divide your money among these asset classes is the first and most important step in building an investment portfolio. In this book, subdivisions of major asset classes are referred to as "subasset classes" or just plain "asset classes." Examples include: Short-Term bonds, Small Cap Value stocks, Emerging Market stocks. (I'll explain these terms in a few minutes.) The categories shown below are the most widely used subasset classes. Together, they come close to representing the entire global securities market.

SUBASSET CLASSES

STOCKS	BONDS
Large-cap value	Money market securities
Large-cap growth	Short-term
Midcap value	Intermediate-term
Midcap growth	Mortgage-backed
International	Tax-exempt
Real estate investment trust (REIT)	Long-term
Small-cap value	International

Small-cap growth   High-yield
Sectors
Emerging market

These subasset classes are arranged, *roughly,* in ascending order of risk—least volatile at the top, most volatile at the bottom. At any given point in a market cycle, the rankings may change, though the classes at the top and bottom of both lists are not likely to budge. Some of these terms may not be familiar to you, so let's see what they mean.

MARKET CAPITALIZATION

The most basic difference among stock subasset classes is market capitalization (cap). It's the price of a company's stock times the number of shares outstanding. Think of it as the price all investors are willing to pay for all of a company's outstanding stock. The size categories for individual stocks—and for mutual funds that hold these stocks—are roughly as follows:

CATEGORY	CAPITALIZATION
Large Cap	Over $7 billion
Mid Cap	$1 billion to $7 billion
Small Cap	Under $500 million to $1 billion
Micro Cap	$50 million to about $300 million

Large Cap funds are the workhorses of investing—sturdy and generally reliable. But you don't expect them to take you anywhere fast. (The mid- to late nineties were a major exception.) Most of the time, Small Caps are the racehorses of investing—fast, temperamental, unpredictable. You could make a lot; you could lose a lot. Mid Cap funds are in between. They usually act like Large Caps, but occasionally, they earn their own place in the sun by galloping past both Large Caps and Small Caps.

GROWTH VERSUS VALUE STOCKS

Another basic difference among asset classes is whether they're "growth" or "value." In a growth fund, you pay a relatively *high* price per unit of the following:

- Company earnings
- Dividends
- Book value (net value of a company's assets)

In a value fund, you pay a relatively *low* price for earnings, dividends, and book value. A value fund emphasizes earnings stability over exciting growth prospects. Whether a fund concentrates on growth or value is referred to as the fund's "style."

Usually, growth funds tend to outperform value funds in up markets, while value funds do better than growth funds in down or flat markets. Over a period of ten years or more, there usually isn't much difference between them; over shorter periods, there can be a significant difference.

OTHER STOCK CLASSES

International usually refers to large-company stocks in *developed* foreign countries, like Germany, France, Japan. *Emerging market* refers to the stocks of companies in *developing* countries—Indonesia, Poland, Brazil. Whether big or small, emerging-market stocks tend to act like highly volatile domestic small caps. *Sector* stocks are those representing only a *single* industry (like health care or financial services) or a *specific group* of industries (like natural resources or technology). They tend to be very volatile. Fortunes have been made—and lost—in sector stocks and funds. When mutual fund returns are compared with each other, sector funds are often excluded because of their specialized nature.

BOND ASSET CLASSES

Federal and corporate bonds are commonly divided into three groups, depending on how long they take to mature:

Short-term: one to three years
Intermediate: up to ten years
Long-term: up to thirty years

Mortgage-backed refers to securities guaranteed as to timely payment of interest and principal by an agency of the federal government. Government National Mortgage Association bonds (Ginnie-Maes) are an example. High-yield bonds are commonly (and unfairly) called "junk bonds." Purchased through a mutual fund, they can offer high return for acceptable risk. There are also international bonds, which often offer higher interest rates.

FUND OBJECTIVES

It's important to distinguish between a fund's *style* and its *objective*. The former refers (mainly) to whether a fund's manager prefers Growth or Value stocks. The latter refers to the investment goal a fund is designed to achieve. Examples of fund objectives include:

Aggressive growth
Growth
Growth and income
Equity income

Mutual funds composed of securities in a specific asset class tend to behave like a group of individual securities in that class. You can, for example, expect a Large Cap value stock fund to be more stable in price than a fund of Emerging Market stocks.

POPULAR INDEXES

Each important asset class tends to have one or more indexes that represent it. Here is a partial list, just to help you become familiar with some of the players:

STOCK INDEXES

LARGE CAP
Standard & Poor's 500 (Growth and Value)
Russell 1,000 (Growth and Value)
Barra Large Cap (Growth and Value)

MID CAP
Standard & Poor's Mid Cap 400 (Growth and Value)
Barra Mid Cap (Growth and Value)

SMALL CAP
Russell 2,000 (Growth and Value)
Wilshire 4,500 (Growth and Value)
Barra Small Cap (Growth and Value)

THE ENTIRE DOMESTIC MARKET
Russell 3,000
Wilshire 5,000

INTERNATIONAL
Morgan Stanley Capital International—Europe, Australasia, and Far East
Morgan Stanley Capital International—Select Emerging Markets (Free Nations)

This list is far from comprehensive. I'm just citing the names often mentioned in financial publications. The numbers, like 3,000 and 5,000, refer to the approximate number of different stocks in the indexes.

BOND INDEXES

SHORT-TERM
Lehman Short-Term

INTERMEDIATE-TERM
Lehman Gov./Corp. Intermediate

LONG-TERM
Lehman Gov./Corp. Long-Term

THE ENTIRE DOMESTIC MARKET
Lehman Aggregate (consists of Long-Term U.S. Treasury
and Investment-Grade Corporate Bonds, Mortgage-
Backed, Federal Government Agency and lower-grade
Corporate)

Again, the list is not comprehensive. There are many kinds of bonds and bond indexes. International bonds are a prime example. It's a matter of how finely you want to slice the pie.

We haven't discussed *cash*, which does not mean literal cash. It's an industry term referring to a variety of Money Market instruments: 30-to-90-day treasury bills (T-bills), short-term treasury notes, and other forms of highly "liquid" securities, such as CDs and corporate short-term debt called "commercial paper." (Liquidity is related to volatility. A highly liquid security tends to hold its market value even during extreme conditions.) In retirement portfolios, short-term bonds are usually liquid enough to be used as cash.

IN BRIEF

The stock and bond markets consist of diverse asset classes that may vary widely in their response to economic and market events. As mentioned earlier, when you compare the performance of two or more mutual funds, it's important to make sure they're in the same asset class. Otherwise, it's apples and oranges.

Fact No. 2. Risk usually determines return

Long term, the markets reward risk. They have to. Why should you take more risk without getting more return? The price of any security represents a precise trade-off between perceived risk and perceived reward. These perceptions can lead to substantial differences in investment return. Example: After adjusting for inflation, the seventy-year return on domestic Small Cap stocks (perceived as risky) is more than *three times higher* than the return on treasury bills (perceived as safe). The return on Large Cap stocks is about twice as high as the return on long-term treasury bonds. (These figures are derived from Ibbotson's *Stocks, Bonds, Bills, and Inflation: 1997 Yearbook.*) The following statements are generally true:

- Short-term money market securities, such as 90-day T-bills, usually don't fluctuate in market value. They're like cash.
- Bonds are stable or risky, depending on the length of time before they mature. The market value of 30-year treasury bonds can sometimes look like a roller-coaster. Generally, though, bonds are less risky than stocks because the interest they pay is not dependent on near-term profits. Also, they tend to pay a higher income in interest than most stocks pay in dividends.
- The volatility of stocks is often (though not invariably) a function of their size and other objective criteria. Big-company stocks tend to be more stable than small-company stocks. Value stocks are more stable than growth stocks. Stocks of developed countries are more stable than those of emerging markets.

There are exceptions to the risk-determines-return rule. (There are always exceptions.) In the mid- to late-nineties, big stocks outperformed small stocks. And during the seventies, there were times when short-term debt produced a higher return than big stocks. But these exceptions prove the rule: The higher the risk, the higher the return. All of which leads to this point:

> You can't judge a fund's return until you know how much risk the manager took to earn it.

Thumb through financial magazines, and you'll see lots of ads that compare a fund's return with that of the S&P 500. This works only if the advertised fund weighs in with the same level of risk as the S&P. If not, the comparison is invalid. The higher-risk fund *should* pay a higher return. Otherwise, investors are not compensated for taking more risk. This principle applies even when the fund compares itself with the average performance of funds in the same asset class. The comparison is misleading if the manager took more risk than his or her peers.

"YES, BUT WHAT IS RISK AND HOW DO YOU MEASURE IT?"

Good questions, because the answers are different for different people. The way you evaluate risk can have a big impact on your investment results.

It turns out there are many ways to define and measure risk. From the average investor's point of view, *risk is the possibility of not having the money you need when you need it.* This definition makes a useful point: Variations in value *before* you need the money are not all that important.

Another word for risk is "volatility." It refers to how much a security or fund has moved up and down in value—the height and depth of the swings. Two commonly used measures of volatility are "beta" and "standard deviation." If you read financial publications even occasionally, you're going to see these terms.

MEASURES OF RISK

Beta: Sets the volatility of an important index (usually the S&P 500) equal to one. Simple arithmetic then tells you how much the volatility of a fund, stock, or portfolio has been above or below that of the S&P. A beta of 1.5, for example, would mean that whatever you're measuring has been 50 percent more volatile than the S&P. Professionals do not consider beta the best measure of risk. I'll spare you the reasons.

Standard deviation: Don't look this up in the dictionary; it will only fog your brain. We civilians can think of it as a sophisticated form of averaging. It measures how much *individual* swings in value vary from the *average of all* swings in value, up and down, within the same set of data. A standard deviation of 10, for example, means that two-thirds of the time, returns have ranged from 10 percent above the average return to 10 percent below it. What's important to remember is that different asset classes have different standard deviations, some high, some low. It works like this:

- *High standard deviation* means a fund tends to have big swings in value. It goes up more than average in bull markets, and goes down more than average in bear markets. Small-cap growth funds, for example, have a high standard deviation.
- *Low standard deviation* means a fund tends to have small swings in value. It does better in bear markets than average, and falls behind in bull markets. Equity income funds, for example, have a low standard deviation.

Standard deviations can vary from period to period. The S&P 500, for example, has varied from a high of twenty-one in the mid-eighties to a low of eight in the early nineties. The average from December 1983, through June 1996 was fourteen. The numbers are useful. If you see a fund with a standard deviation of twenty, you can expect it to do better in an up market than the

S&P 500. The reverse would be true for a fund with a standard deviation of eight.

As you might expect, there is a technique for factoring out risk. It's called the "Sharpe ratio," after the Nobel laureate who invented it, William Sharpe. One version of his formula is simple. You take the return on 90-day treasury bills and subtract it from the fund's return. Then divide the result by the fund's standard deviation. (The treasury bill return is subtracted to reflect what an investor can get with little or no risk.)

$$\frac{20\% \text{ fund return minus } 4\% \text{ risk-free return}}{14\% \text{ standard deviation of the fund}} = 1.14\% \text{ risk-adjusted return}$$

When you see the term "risk-adjusted return" in publications, it usually refers to the Sharpe ratio.

Condition of the markets: Strictly speaking, this is neither a measure of risk, nor a gauge of your capacity to assume risk. But it's often used to decide how much risk a person should take *at a point in time.* This implies an ability to time the markets. You know the story on that. Even an objective "predictor" like dividend yield is not reliable. For decades, it was understood that dividend yield is an important part of the return on stocks and that, further, if the yield on large stocks drops below 3 percent, stocks are bound to do poorly. That was the conventional wisdom. From the mid- to late nineties, large stocks ignored the rule. Rising prices drove the dividend yield down to less than 2 percent, confounding many experts.

Past versus future risk: The downside of all measures of past risk is that the past may not repeat. If a fund makes substantial changes in the kinds of asset classes it holds, its future risk will change. To cite a well-known case, Fidelity Magellan fund in 1995 substantially lowered its risk (and return) when it switched a large part of its portfolio from stocks to bonds.

Standard deviation is the standard: Most investors are not equipped to track and evaluate changes in a fund's asset classes.

So where does that leave us in terms of selecting a way to measure risk? For this book, I think it leaves us with standard deviation, which provides a measure of price movements, both up and down. Standard deviation can be used for all kinds of funds, regardless of asset class. It's the measure most commonly used in investment publications—and the one you'll usually see when mutual fund rates of return are compared.

CATEGORIES OF RISK

In addition to different *measures* of risk, there are also different *categories* of risk. Here are some you should know about:

- *Market risk.* The most important category of risk is fluctuations in the price of a security, fund, or portfolio.
- *Manager risk.* This term refers to the fact that fund managers make mistakes. In fact, the average manager of diversified equity funds is usually off the mark when it comes to picking stocks and timing trades. That's one of the reasons he or she has failed to match the fund's relevant index fund.
- *Currency risk.* Fluctuations in return caused by changing currency exchange rates. This is a bit tricky. If you buy a French security (stock or bond), and it goes up in its quoted price, you don't necessarily have a paper profit. The rise in the value of the security in francs may be offset by a rise in the value of the dollar versus the franc. This means each franc is translated into fewer dollars, so the U.S. investor gets a lower return.
- *Credit risk.* Refers to bonds only. It's the possibility that the organization you've loaned money to will fail to pay your interest on time, or even fail to refund the face amount of the bond when it's due for payment.

IN BRIEF

Risk has a variety of meanings and categories. The most commonly used measure is standard deviation, a sophisticated form of averaging. There are also various categories of risk, the most important of which is change in market value.

Fact No. 3. *Average return depends on which period you measure*

This is a big one. Exaggerating a bit, a fund can demonstrate any return it wants by the time period it chooses to measure. The tables below (courtesy of Vanguard and Standard & Poor's) make the point.

DECADE	AVERAGE ANNUAL RETURNS: S&P 500 (%)
1930s	-.1
1940s	9.2
1950s	19.4

With the return growing by huge amounts, you might be inclined to think the S&P 500 is a rocket to riches. Things change when you look further.

1950s	19.4
1960s	7.8
1970s	5.9

Now it appears the S&P 500 is bound for the bottom—clearly a poor investment. But the 1980s saw the return leap to 17.5 percent. Where it will be at the end of the nineties is anybody's guess.

Even a few days can make a difference. Remember when the Dow fell off a cliff on October 19, 1987? Assume a fund opened for business on October 20. Fast forward ten years, and you're likely to have an outstanding return; the fund bought into the markets when stocks were cheap. Change the start date to October 18, and the ten-year return is apt to be much lower. This sort of arithmetic is built into a fund's long-term performance. When a fund brags about its record "since inception," check where the markets were when the fund started.

Less obvious, but also misleading, is what many non-index funds do at the end of every calendar year. An article by Jason Zweig in the November 1997 issue of *Money* is headlined, "Watch out for the Year-End Fund Flimflam." Drawing on a study, Zweig documents how year-end "window dressing" (essentially, accounting tricks) can transform a lagging fund into an index-beater on the last business day of the year. Worse, guess what happened to the average fund that pulled this trick. It lost all it had gained on the last day of Year 1 on the first day of Year 2. From loser to winner to loser, all in two business days.

THE PROFESSIONAL SOLUTION: ROLLING TIME PERIODS

When you measure only one time period in a fund's record, you probably won't get a typical figure. Professionals deal with this problem by using a method called "rolling time periods." Instead of simply measuring, say, the five-year period, 1994–1998, they measure *every* five-year period over a selected time span. This gives them a range of average annual returns, and a more accurate picture of how a fund has performed. As you'll see, I recommend that funds provide rolling time periods in their sales brochures and prospectuses.

Fact No. 4. Stocks usually go up

Stocks go up, stocks go down, but mostly they go up. In fact, up years outnumber down years by about three to one. Think of the possibilities. You could train a parrot that, when asked what the stock market will do, would always answer, "Go up." Three-quarters of the time (long term), the parrot would be right. With that kind of record—and given the power of media hype—it might not be long before the parrot became a popular stock market guru. Moral: Don't be overly impressed by a fund's growth rate over time; most of that growth probably came simply from owning stocks.

SUMMARY

We've just reviewed four facts to consider when evaluating any fund's return, index or non-index:

1. Stock and bond markets consist of diverse asset classes, which have different risk and return characteristics.
2. Rate of return tends to be proportional to risk. Most investment professionals use standard deviation—a form of averaging swings in value—to measure risk. Market risk is the most important of several categories of risk.
3. The time period selected for measurement can make a big difference in a fund's apparent record. Professionals use rolling time periods.
4. Since 1926, the domestic stock markets have gone up in three years out of four.

You are now in a much better position to evaluate the performance of index funds versus non-index funds, which happens to be our next topic.

CHAPTER 5

Fund Returns:
Index Versus Non-index

Now that you know something about judging fund returns, we can get to the business of comparing the records of index funds with those of non-index funds. At this point—if you've been paying attention—you may be inclined to object:

> Hold it! You've said several times that the past does not predict. Why are we going to look at the past now?

Because this situation is different. We're not comparing funds with funds. We're comparing two entirely different approaches to investing. One has *inherent* advantages over the other, including lower costs, lower tax structure, and relative predictability. *These advantages do not depend on what's happening in the markets or the economy;* they are part of a defining difference between index and non-index investing. Since these differences are permanent and significant, I think it's fair to review what those differences have produced in the past.

DON'T BE MISLED BY GROSS RETURNS

Let's start by looking at the *gross* returns of stock funds and bond funds. For two reasons: It's a familiar way to compare returns, and it sets up a logical point: If indexing can win on a gross basis, it can obviously rout the competition on a net basis. "Gross" refers to the numbers you see in financial publications. They're gross because they don't reflect various subtractors, such as *sales charges* (which reduce your cash return) and *excess risk* (which reduces your adjusted return).

When you do the homework on gross returns, you find that indexing wins in a broad variety of asset classes and time periods. If you'd like to check this out for yourself, go to any large business library and make a specific request: You want to see the average performance of "actively managed" (non-index) funds by asset class (not the performance of individual funds). At the same time, you want to compare each asset class with its relevant index (not just the S&P 500). Finally, you want these data for a variety of time periods—three, five, ten, and fifteen years. You will find that again and again, indexing wins, *even on a gross basis.*

For more on this subject, go to Vanguard's Web site (www.vanguard.com) and find "The Implications of Style Analysis on Mutual Fund Performance Evaluation" by John C. Bogle. The subtitle is "TIC-TAC-TOE"; we cover part of the work later in this chapter.

There have been, and always will be, times when a gross fund average beats the index in its asset class. But no one knows *when* those times will occur. And no one knows *which* funds will beat their index benchmark. *Result: There's no practical way to take advantage of the times when non-index funds win.* (Please let me know if you figure out a reliable way to overcome this problem. I'd much rather be rich than right.)

BELIEVE IN NET RETURNS

Net returns take you from the let's-pretend world of published returns into the real world of how much money your funds may put in your wallet. The key to making this switch is to compare apples with apples. Example: Suppose you want to compare the returns of two Small Cap funds, one index and the other non-index. Before you can make a valid comparison, you need to ask at least six questions:

1. Does the non-index fund have a sales charge? If so, how much will it cost you over (say) ten years?
2. Does the non-index fund have a much higher turnover than the index fund? If so, how much will you have to pay in additional capital gains taxes?
3. Looking ahead ten years, how much extra will you have to pay because the non-index fund has higher operating and transaction costs? (The usual difference is seven to ten times more.)
4. Does the non-index fund have a higher risk level than the index fund?
5. Has the non-index fund engaged in style drift?
6. Suppose you're comparing the average return of a class of non-index funds with a relevant index. How far does the non-index return fall when you adjust for survivorship bias?

Let's see what happens when we translate some of these questions into actual numbers.

Costs

Costs make a bigger difference than many investors realize. Take sales charges, for example. Assume you invest $10,000, with an effective load of 6 percent and an average total return of 10 percent. The arithmetic of negative compounding reveals a chilling fact: In less than thirty years, *the dollar amount you lose will exceed your original investment.* That happens because you lose the 10 percent annual growth on the $600 in sales charges. Who could blame you for asking, "Is the service I'll get from the salesperson worth that kind of money?" That question is especially relevant when you remember you could probably earn a higher return with an index fund.

Less obvious is the impact of operating costs, which, for the average diversified non-index stock fund, amount to 1.5 percent. Add that to an estimated .5 percent in average transaction costs, which are also a drain on return. You now have a total cost of 2 percentage points *every year.* How hard does that hit? Vanguard's John Bogle provides an answer in a speech called "The Four Dimensions of Investment Return," given at a 1998 forum sponsored by the Institute for Private Investors. He points out that over a twenty-five-year period, a $1,000,000 investment returning 10 percent would grow to $10.8 million; the same amount invested at 8 percent would total only $6.8 million. Operating and transaction costs would have consumed $4 million of your money.

Taxes

You may recall that index funds have much lower turnover rates than do non-index funds—around 5 percent, compared with an average of 85 percent (and running to more than 200 percent). Assuming a taxable account, this is why index funds generate much lower capital gains distributions. Dixon and Shoven (chapter 3) found that investors in the highest tax brackets keep only

45 percent of the returns from taxable accounts reported by non-index funds. People in midrange brackets lose less, but the loss to taxes is still substantial.

Risk

We know it's misleading to compare the performance of funds with different degrees of risk (standard deviation). But how does that translate into actual numbers? In a 1998 paper called "Tic-Tac-Toe" (adapted from a speech given at a Morningstar conference in 1997), John Bogle provides an illuminating answer for three asset classes. Part of his study (as summarized in "Appendix B") covers the five-year period, December 31, 1991, through December 31, 1996. The following figures are adapted from his data and rounded for simplicity.

Average Annual Returns:

NON-INDEX FUNDS VERSUS
ADJUSTED INDEX

Fund average	Adjusted index	Index advantage
Large Cap		
13%	17%	27%
Mid Cap		
14	18	30
Small Cap		
15	20	29

"Adjusted index" means that the risk (volatility) of the index is adjusted to equal the average risk of the funds. It answers the question, "How high would the index be if it had the same risk as the average non-index fund?"

Two things stand out: (1) The index holds an advantage of at least 20 percent in *each* asset class. And (2) *the largest advantage for indexing comes with Small Cap stocks.* In this example, the average Small Cap manager didn't perform better than the index; he or she simply took more risk. And risk is like a mean-tempered dog: There's always a chance it will come back and bite you.

Survivorship bias

This effect can be substantial, as Malkiel has pointed out. For a fifteen-year period, the average return on *surviving* diversified equity funds was 18.7 percent (chapter 3). When *all* funds were counted, including *non*-survivors, the figure fell to 14.5 percent. *This means that non-index equity fund returns were overstated by 22 percent.* This kind of effect applies to asset classes like those we just reviewed; it does not apply to individual funds.

NET RETURN SUMMARY

We've looked at several factors that affect the useful return on mutual funds. To the best of my knowledge, there is no academic study that quantifies the *combined* effect of all these factors. Until someone produces such a study, we can only go by common sense. From that vantage point—and referring to money in taxable accounts—I believe the following is a reasonable guess:

> The study will show that index funds have outperformed non-index funds on a net basis in every asset class, over every time period of three or more years. Any exceptions will be the result of style drift.

> This is crucial. You don't put your kids through college or provide for your retirement with statistics. You do it with dollars—the money you can spend *after* adjusting gross returns for survivorship bias and differences in sales charges, costs, taxes, and risk.

WHAT ABOUT BEAR MARKETS?

There is a theory, proclaimed as gospel in some financial publications, that goes something like this:

> Yes, index funds do well in up markets, but not in down markets. That's when you'll see the actively managed (non-index) funds really shine, because they have cash reserves, which they are free to keep at any level. When it looks like the market's going south, they can increase their cash holdings to cushion the blow. Index funds don't hold cash, so they're going to be hit a lot harder when the markets go down.

That's the theory. The actuality is a whole other thing, for these reasons:

1. The average non-index fund holds very little cash

The New York Times reported on June 26, 1996, that the *most* cash the average stock fund held from 1984 through June, 1996, was about 12 percent. The *average* amount was about 9 percent. That small percentage in cash is not going to make much difference in the fund's resistance to a down market. Nor is that average percentage likely to change by much. Managers get paid for performance, not for treading water. They can't afford to have a significant portion of their fund miss an upturn in the markets.

2. Non-index fund managers can't predict the future

Holding cash as a protection against a bear market implies that non-index fund managers can predict what the markets will do. They can't. Scientific studies have shown that there's no reliable way to time the markets, not even if you're a Great Predictor. In *A Random Walk Down Wall Street*, Burton Malkiel shows two charts (from Goldman Sachs) that make the point. During the 1970s and 1980s, fund managers held relatively little cash when they should have held a lot, and a lot when they should have held a little. The alleged benefit of holding cash disappears in a cloud of smoke.

3. The record shows that the S&P 500 index maintains an advantage over non-index funds during down markets

A study by Lipper Analytical Services compares six different kinds of funds with the S&P 500:

Capital Appreciation	Equity Income
Growth	Growth and Income
Mid Cap	Small Company Growth

The study defines a down market as a negative move of 10 percent from the last turning point, as measured on the Lipper Growth Fund Index. Data are provided for six down markets, from August 31, 1978, through October 11, 1990. Result: The S&P 500 comes out ahead.

Average loss in the S&P 500:	15.12%
Average loss in non-index funds:	17.04%

On average, the non-index funds went down 12.7 percent *more* than the S&P 500. The difference to investors would be slightly less because an S&P 500 *fund* has operating expenses of .2 percent or .3 percent.

Beating the *average* fund in down markets does not mean the S&P beat *all* funds. An asset class with a lower standard deviation than the S&P 500 would be expected to do better than the S&P 500. And in fact, this was the case. Equity Income, the most conservative asset class in the study, went down only 10.38 percent on the Lipper index. Of course, there's a price to pay for this stability. Equity Income lags the S&P 500 during bull markets. In short, index funds in six recent down markets held up just as well as—or better than—non-index funds.

THE ADVANTAGES OF
INDEX FUNDS, REVIEWED

We've seen that index funds have outperformed non-index funds in a range of asset classes, over different periods, and in down markets, as well as up. For convenience, let's review the reasons all in one place:

1. Better gross performance,
for both stocks and bonds

Just one example: For the fifteen-year period, ending June 30, 1998, low-cost S&P 500 index funds outperformed 84 percent of their non-index rivals. Bond index funds also outperformed bond non-index funds during the same period.

2. An even better record of net performance

After deducting for survivorship bias and other subtractors (higher taxes, costs, risk, and sales charges where they apply), index funds are likely to outperform their non-index rivals by significant margins in every asset class, including Small Cap stocks. This advantage is likely to continue for the reasons discussed here.

3. Lower capital gains taxes

The average non-index stock fund has a high turnover, replacing about 85 percent of its securities every twelve months. Some aggressive funds have turnovers of more than 200 percent. Every time the fund sells a security that's gone up in price, it generates a capital gains tax distribution—and capital gains taxes. In contrast, a typical index fund has a turnover of less than 5 percent. This means that nearly all the capital gains can be deferred, rather than distributed.

4. Lower operating costs for both stocks and bond funds

Expenses *and* transaction costs for the average *stock* non-index fund run about *ten times* higher than those of their index rivals (2 percent versus .2 percent). Expenses and transaction costs for the average *bond* non-index fund average about 5.6 times higher (1.02 percent versus .18 percent for its index counterpart). Low costs give index funds a persistent advantage, year after year, in up markets and down.

5. Relative predictability (sleep better)

When you buy a *non*-index fund, you have no idea of how it will do against its peers or a relevant index. In contrast, you know—beyond any doubt—that an index fund will match its relevant index (minus operating costs and any tracking error). You also know that it's likely to outperform the average non-index fund in its asset class. In the roller-coaster world of investing, that's peace of mind.

6. Better diversification

In a non-index fund, you own what a Great Predictor thinks you should own. Which means your money could be broadly diversified—or concentrated in stocks that tend to move together in response to the same events. The second situation gives you the potential for big gains. Or big losses. Which may be fine, if you're willing to accept that much risk. Otherwise, you're better off in an index fund, where you own *all* the securities that meet specific objective criteria.

7. Always fully invested

One of the most dangerous mutual fund myths is that non-index managers have an advantage in bear markets: They can go to cash. This alleged advantage hasn't found its way into the real world. The record shows that index funds (or at least the S&P 500) have done just as well as non-index funds in bear markets.

Beyond that, we've learned that market timing doesn't work. That's especially true when you bet *against* the markets. The stock markets have gone up in three out of four years for more than fifty years. Finally, we know that the markets tend to reward risk. It stands to reason that if you shield your money from potential losses, you also shield it from potential gains.

8. No manager risk

All investing involves some degree of risk. When you buy a non-index fund, *you increase that risk:* The manager may make mistakes in judgment. Since the average non-index manager has lagged behind his or her relevant index, that risk is substantial.

9. No style drift

When you buy a non-index fund, you don't necessarily get what you think you're buying. The manager may engage in style drift—buying securities that do not meet the fund's stated objective. A Small Cap fund, for example, may own a significant percentage of Mid Cap securities. This makes it hard for this kind of fund to play a definite role in your portfolio.

10. A wide range of choices

This is not an advantage that index funds have over non-index. But the S&P 500 has had so much press lately, it's easy to forget there are index funds for practically every asset class you can think of. You've got all the raw material you need to build an all-index portfolio composed entirely of index funds (see Malkiel's model portfolios in chapter 14).

11. User-friendly

Compared with non-index funds, index funds are easier to evaluate and easier to track. This is no small thing. There are more than 8,000 mutual funds out there. How do you decide which ones to buy? Past performance? We know that doesn't work. We also know there are all sorts of techniques funds can use to overstate their returns. So there you are, staring at columns of numbers, thinking, "Yes, but what do they all mean?" Not so with index funds; what you see is what you get. For the same reasons, index funds are easier to monitor. Life can be simple.

12. No sales charges

If you hunt around, you can find index funds with a sales charge. But most are no-loads. In contrast, 50 percent to 60 percent of non-index stock funds and 33 percent of taxable bond funds hit you with a sales charge ranging from 3 percent to 6 percent. That's on top of their average operating and transaction costs of about 2 percent. In a 10,000-meter run, non-index funds start at least a lap behind.

INDEX FUNDS ATTACKED

We've seen the case *for* index funds. In all fairness, we should look at the case *against* index funds. And, to be objective, it should be presented by an advocate of non-index funds. With that in mind, I searched for a source cloaked in the mantle of prestige. I may have found it in *Forbes,* widely regarded as the most prestigious big-circulation business magazine. An article in the April 1997 issue attacks index funds on at least six major points, *all of them wrong:*

1. *It equates indexing with buying the S&P 500.* In fact, as we've seen, you can buy index funds in a wide range of asset classes. It makes no sense to put down indexing because one asset class may be overvalued at a particular time.
2. *It claims the fact that "the S&P 500 usually beats active management" is a myth.* Sounds of raucous laughter.
3. *It claims that the S&P beats Small Cap stocks only rarely.* As we've seen, this is simply not true, even on a gross basis. On a net basis, it's not even close to being true.
4. *It frets about what the S&P will do to Value investors*—but neglects to point out you can buy index funds consisting entirely of Value stocks.
5. *It worries that "investors who buy and hold index funds can never rebalance their holdings."* What? Rebalancing index funds is as easy as rebalancing non-index funds. You sell the asset classes that exceed your target percentage and use the money to buy undertarget asset classes.
6. *It fails to point out that the net returns of non-index funds can be much lower than their gross returns, as reviewed in this chapter.*

It's a mystery to me how the competent editors of *Forbes* allowed this article to appear with all these (rather obvious) errors. If this is the strongest attack America's most prestigious business magazine can make on indexing, I think we're on solid ground.

SUMMARY

1. Index funds have outperformed non-index funds in a wide range of asset classes and time periods.
2. Index funds take an even bigger lead over non-index funds on a *net* basis—when returns are adjusted for survivorship bias and differences in sales charges, costs, taxes, risk, and types of securities held.
3. Low-cost S&P 500 index funds have held up during bear markets just as well as non-index funds. The alleged advantages of holding cash are more theoretical than real.
4. Index funds have at least twelve advantages over non-index funds, including generally better performance.
5. People who attack indexing don't necessarily use valid arguments.

CHAPTER 6

Does the Past Predict?

I hear a voice:

> Index funds are for losers. I don't care if they beat the average non-index fund. Because I'm not going to buy the average. I'm going to buy the best, and only the best. There are lots of newsletters and magazines that tell you which funds had the highest return for the quarter, the year, or whatever time you want. I'll just buy the winners and leave your index funds behind in the dust.

Is the voice right? Is it really that easy to get rich? If so, why isn't everybody doing it? These questions raise the issue of whether or not the past performance of a non-index fund is predictive. To put it another way, can you beat the markets by betting on the record of the Great Predictors?

My co-author, Burton Malkiel, gave us the short answer in

his Introduction: "For all practical purposes, no." But the issue deserves a closer look. Personal finance publications bombard us with news about the latest covey of high-flying non-index funds. On top of that come the advertisements—page after page of funds bragging about their track records. The average reader could be forgiven for inferring that past results *must* predict future results. Otherwise, why all the fuss? When you press purveyors of past performance for evidence, they talk about a few scholarly studies that seem to support their claims—until you look at the studies closely. Let's do that.

FOUR STUDIES OF PRICE PERSISTENCE

We're going to move through a range of findings, starting with a study that reports the strongest evidence of "performance persistence" (winners and losers repeating).

1. There was a period when the past predicted, and there were complex ways to profit from it

In the July 1996 issue of *The Journal of Finance*, Martin Gruber published an article entitled, "Another Puzzle: The Growth in Actively Managed Mutual Funds." Gruber is chair of the finance department at New York University's Stern School of Business. He studied the period 1985–1994, using an initial data set of 270 funds.

Gruber reports strong evidence of winners repeating, *provided* a certain complex procedure is followed. He shows that for the period studied, there were ways to gain an annual risk-adjusted edge of three-quarters of a percentage point over relevant indexes by buying a group of recent top performers. He also shows that at least some investors were able to profit by following these steps:

1. Buy the top 10 percent of the top-ranked funds. Using Gruber's initial data set, that's twenty-seven funds.
2. Select these funds by using something called "four-index alphas" or a reasonable approximation.
3. Turn over the entire portfolio—all twenty-seven funds—once a year.
4. Select new funds only from the original list of 270.
5. In taxable portfolios, do not hold the funds beyond certain periods determined by tax bracket.

The reported gain is available *only* by following this procedure. In addition, Gruber's study confirms that S&P 500 index funds outperformed the average diversified non-index stock fund during the period studied. He also finds that investors in load funds fared worse than those in no-load funds. His study accounts for survivorship bias and taxes, but not for sales charges.

Using Gruber's study, another investigator finds partial support of Gruber's findings, but comes to a different conclusion:

> The trading strategies, however, suggest that for the whole sample there are no significant gains from constructing a portfolio of funds with positive new money. The new money is smart mainly because it leaves the poorly-performing funds. For the whole sample, there is no significant evidence that active investors in general can beat the market.
>
> "Is Money Smart?," Lu Zheng,
> *Journal of Finance*, 1998.

2. The past predicted during a certain period, but that won't necessarily do you much good

William Goetzmann and Roger Ibbotson published an article called "Do Winners Repeat?" in a 1994 issue of *The Journal of Portfolio Management*. Goetzmann was assistant professor of finance at the Columbia University Graduate School of Business. Ibbotson is professor in practice at the Yale School of Management and president of Ibbotson Associates, a leading mutual fund research firm. They worked with a data base that grew from 258 funds from the beginning of 1976 to 728 mutual funds at the end of 1988. Among their findings:

- The top 25 percent of funds from the initial period has by far the best results in later periods.
- These results are not available simply by buying a few top performers; the pattern applies only to buying the entire top 25 percent. In this study that's seventy-three funds.
- The winners-repeat pattern is not necessarily a guide to beating the S&P 500 index, but does appear to be a guide to beating long-term fund averages.
- The pattern is inconsistent in the short term and may represent higher return because of higher risk.
- The strongest evidence of price persistence came from poor performers—losers are likely to remain losers. This finding reinforced the results of an earlier Goetzmann study.

The study's results do not reflect sales charges or taxes and only partly account for survivorship bias—factors that can make a big difference in net return.

3. The past may have predicted, but the evidence is inconclusive

In March 1995, William F. Sharpe published a paper on the internet (http://wsharpe.stanford.edu): "The Styles and Performance of Large, Seasoned U.S. Mutual Funds, 1985–1994." Sharpe is a Nobel laureate and professor of economics in the Graduate School of Business at Stanford University. The following summarizes the portion of his paper entitled, "The Performance of Subsets of the LS 100 Funds, 1985–1994."

To measure the predictive value of past performance, Sharpe worked with the top-performing twenty-five large funds each year from 1985 through 1994. When he used the prior twelve months as a guide to future prices, he found that, on average, these twenty-five winners outperformed the one hundred largest mutual funds by .48 percent per year for both five-year and ten-year periods. The predictive value dropped when he used the prior twenty-four months and thirty-six months. He closes with a caution:

> However, closer examination of the record of the last two or three years could lead to at least a neutral position on the issues. Either way, the evidence [for winners repeating] is far from conclusive, statistically or economically.

Sharpe's study accounts for differences in risk, but does not consider the impact of sales charges or taxes.

4. You're better off with index funds

The June 1995 issue of *The Journal of Finance* carried an article by Burton Malkiel entitled, "Returns from Investing in Equity Mutual Funds, 1971 to 1991."

Malkiel worked with a unique data set free of survivorship bias: Group performance was not inflated by the elimination of funds that failed. Working with a set of 239 funds over twenty-one years, he made several key discoveries:

- *Survivorship bias substantially lowered the performance of the group of funds in his study.* Malkiel covers this point in his introduction.
- *From 1971 through 1991, the evidence for the predictability of non-index mutual fund returns is mixed.* Malkiel reports that winners tended to repeat almost two-thirds of the time during the seventies and part of the eighties.

... there seems to be considerable persistence to returns during the 1970s. Hot hands (winning followed by winning) occur much more often than a win followed by a loss.... Similarly, the data indicate a "cold hand" phenomenon as well. Losing in the initial period is more likely to be followed by losing in the subsequent period.

But this finding does not mean a pattern of winners repeating in one period will continue into another. Things changed considerably during the eighties and early nineties. Malkiel reports:

Over the whole period of the 1980s, it is hard to conclude there is much predictability in mutual fund returns. Winners tended to repeat just over half of the time. Especially after 1986, a period not included in some of the earlier empirical work, winners do especially poorly.... This suggests that persistence may be a phenomenon that existed in the past, but may have later disappeared. [Goetzmann and Ibbotson made similar suggestions.]

Malkiel's most telling example of persistence failing may be his analysis of the *Forbes* "Honor Roll" funds. It takes more than a high ten-year return to qualify for the Honor Roll. A fund has to meet a list of consistency requirements, including good performance in down markets. This process weeds out highly volatile funds that happened to score well at the end of a given measuring period. Malkiel examines the Honor Roll funds from 1976 though 1991. The result:

Buying Forbes Honor Roll funds in the early years, we do achieve well-above average ... rates of return. As the strategy continues, however, investors received well-*below* average returns. Thus, even before considering load fees [and taxes], the strategy of buying good-performing funds does not appear to be a long-run consistent winner.

Malkiel did not stop with the Honor Roll funds. As mentioned in the Introduction, he tried many different methods that have been alleged to produce over-index results. In his words:

> None of a variety of reasonable persistence strategies would have allowed an investor to beat the market during the 1980s, even assuming away the existence of sales fees and load charges. . . . It does not appear that one can fashion a dependable strategy of generating excess returns based on a belief that long-run mutual fund returns are persistent.

Some scholarly studies report that a method may produce a statistical advantage, but fail to work in terms of earning a net profit. Malkiel's findings reinforce this distinction:

> . . . even when the strategy "worked" during the 1970s, an investor could not have achieved the simulated returns because many of the best-performing funds had "load" (sales) charges of up to eight percent of asset value, and the simulated strategies call for switching into the best-performing funds at periodic intervals. Finally, it is important to remember that the persistence results are influenced by survivorship bias.

For taxable accounts, the net return is further reduced by capital gains taxes. Malkiel sums up as follows:

> Most investors would be considerably better off by purchasing a low-expense index fund, than by trying to select active fund managers who appear to possess a "hot hand." Since active management fails to provide excess returns and tends to generate greater tax burdens for investors, the advantage of passive management holds.

Malkiel also reports that buying highly volatile funds did not necessarily bring superior returns. In his words, "There is no evidence that investors seeking higher returns will find the purchase of high-beta mutual funds a strategy that will dependably satisfy their objectives." What this means to you and me is that we won't necessarily get rich just by buying funds labeled "aggressive growth" or "maximum capital appreciation." The markets reward risk; they reward prudence even more.

WHAT HAVE WE LEARNED?

Prompted by self-interest, many Wall Street people jump to conclusions when they hear about a scholarly study that seems to support the winners-repeat theory. A closer look may lead to different conclusions. You can use the following questions as a reality test:

1. *Is the over-index gain significant?* Often, a reported method yields only a small gain, even before taxes and sales charges.
2. *Did the reported method beat a relevant index?* This point comes up a lot in financial publications. We're told that a particular manager beat the average manager in his or her asset class. We're often *not* told whether he or she also beat a relevant index, which is usually a higher hurdle.
3. *Does the reported gain reflect relevant subtractors?* These include capital gains taxes (up to 39.6 percent), sales charges (3 percent to 6 percent), and transaction charges (which are estimated at .5 percent).
4. *Is there a net gain after subtractors?* By the time you subtract higher taxes, sales charges, and higher transaction costs from a small gain—not to mention higher fees to your accountant—do you still come out ahead?
5. *Can people who invest on their own apply the reported methods?* As you've seen, some of the methods used are so elaborate

and demanding that the average investor has little hope of putting them into practice.

6. *Can people who invest through an employer's plan apply the reported methods?* Many price persistence methods (including those described here) require the freedom to choose among thousands of funds. The typical defined contribution (401(k)) plan offers fewer than ten funds.

7. *Is the method practical for buy-and-hold investors?* Many price persistence strategies call for frequent trading with a large number of funds—impossible for a buy-and-hold investor.

8. *Will the method continue to work in the future?* This is fundamental. There is evidence that even genuine patterns of price persistence exist only for certain periods and then disappear. There's no way of knowing if a particular pattern will ever succeed again.

The next time you read about a method of beating the markets, apply this eight-question test. You're more than likely to find the method flunks. And even if it works for some people some of the time, it must eventually fail. By now you know why: If a certain pattern of investing succeeds, other fund managers quickly learn about it and invest the same way. This puts buying pressure on prices and drives them up to the point where the method is no longer profitable. There is, maybe, sometimes, a free snack, but there is no free lunch.

SUMMARY

Based on four scholarly articles dealing with the persistence of mutual fund returns, we've learned:

1. Of four attempts to find a method of price persistence, two are impractical for the average investor, a third finds the re-

sults far from conclusive, and the fourth finds that methods of achieving price persistence do not persist over time.

2. Several studies have reported over-index results by simulating trading dozens of funds at frequent intervals—every year or even every quarter. But the gains are small, and the methods impractical.

3. Survivorship bias substantially overstates the returns of groups of funds.

4. From 1971 through 1991, buying highly volatile funds did not bring superior results.

5. Winners repeated during the seventies and early eighties, but not since.

6. Even when a persistence method "worked" during the seventies, the advantage disappeared after allowing for survivorship bias, sales charges, and taxes.

7. An eight-point set of questions can be used to test the usefulness of methods of price persistence investing.

We've just looked at the structure we're building. Rocks have been thrown at it, but I don't see any dents. We can move ahead knowing that average investors can't improve their net results by buying past performance.

CHAPTER 7

Why Can't Non-Index Funds Do Better?

Consider the Great Predictor we met in Chapter 2. He has multiple degrees from the right schools. He's very bright. He works hard. And he's paid a princely sum. Yet he hasn't earned his income. In fact, fund managers in general don't earn their incomes. Why not? I see at least ten reasons:

1. THEY TRY TO PREDICT THE FUTURE

Perhaps the most basic reason is one that is rarely mentioned: Nobody can predict the future. When a fund manager buys a security, *he or she is making a prediction*. That person is saying, in effect, "The price of this security will rise by a significant amount after I buy it." Similarly, when the manager sells a security, the prediction is, "The price will hold or go down after I sell it." How do managers know these things? They don't. Homo sapiens is not sapient enough to predict the future. In the stock markets, especially, there are just too many things that can change. And even a small change can make a big difference in price. That's why a manager who outperforms his or her relevant index in one market environment fails in another.

2. THEY CAN'T TIME THE MARKETS

This follows from the first point. If you can't reliably predict the future price of a stock, you probably can't predict the future price of an asset class. Every investment newsletter I've seen brags about its ability to time the market. Many fund managers claim they can do it. Revered gurus in giant brokerage firms and investment banking houses imply they can do it.

The truth? Nobody can do it. Economists have studied this subject to death, and the answer is always the same: There is no scientific evidence that anyone can reliably time the markets well enough to make a significant profit after trading costs. Plenty of people *seem* to have done it. They proudly point to famous calls they made just before a big turn in the markets. They also refer to highly sophisticated (and often secret) software models that "have made the right calls for the last 20 years." Don't believe it. In *A Random Walk Down Wall Street,* my co-author Burton Malkiel reports:

> Mutual fund managers have been incorrect in their allocation of assets into cash in essentially every market cycle during the Seventies and Eighties. . . . Clearly the ability of mutual fund managers to time the market has been egregiously poor.

One Great Predictor called the 1987 crash and has been living off that call ever since. The breathless promotional copy for this person's newsletter says,

> called every major market top and bottom within 4%–8% since 1982 . . . has successfully predicted—and avoided— every bear-market crash of the last 20 years. Every single one, with zero false alarms.

With that kind of ability, a person should be able to deliver thrilling performance as a fund manager. Did this happen? Not even close. The November 3, 1996, issue of *The New York Times* showed the results of a sector fund managed by this Great Predictor. The headline for the performance graph says it all: "A Lackluster History." The fund gained an underwhelming 4.8 percent per year from the fall of 1987 through the summer of 1994, when the fund was merged out of existence.

Despite overwhelming contrary evidence, thousands of people believe there are ways to predict the markets. Why is there such a huge gulf between fact and fantasy?

A primary reason is that people tend to believe what they want to believe. It's no surprise, then, that some investors want to believe there's a way to get rich quicker than the rest of us can. Feeding that hunger, market timers use at least nine techniques to support their self-proclaimed ability:

1. It's a group effort

With thousands of Great Predictors making predictions, some of them are bound to be right, some of the time, just by chance. They may become famous when that happens, but they can't sustain their accuracy.

2. They make frequent revisions

Let's go back to the mutual fund company you and I started. We want to add market timing to our sales promotion so we can attract more investors. Don't worry about the fact that we can't predict anything. We get around that little problem by saying "up" at one point in time and "down" at another, or the reverse. We call it a "revised forecast." Sounds official. We can even embellish this technique by forecasting different amounts of up or down. One of them is bound to be close. We choose that one to talk about and forget the others. Who's going to invest the time and money to keep track of our forecasts? Not the SEC; it's perfectly legal to make contradictory predictions. Not our investors; they don't have the time or share of mind. Not our competitors, either; they're all doing the same thing.

3. They fudge

People who do this stuff for a living are very adept at saying things in a way that lets them claim victory, no matter what the market does. It's easy. You just avoid flat-out predictions. You imply, you qualify, you use words like "if," and "could," and "might." You write opaque, convoluted sentences with ambiguous meanings. Then, when you refer to your "prediction," you conveniently fail to mention the words that made your statement an expression of possibility, not a prediction. Example: A stock market guru was asked, "What is your long-term outlook for the stock market?" His answer: "Absent any dramatic changes, huge cash flows into stocks should continue." Absent any dramatic changes? But that's the whole point. Take away change, and you or I could predict the markets.

4. They postpone victory

A market guru who writes for a major financial magazine had a problem. He had to deal with the fact that the bear market he predicted for the fall of 1996 turned out to be a bull market. He wasn't just wrong: he was 180 degrees wrong. But never mind. He handled that little problem by asserting that he was right, and that his prediction will come true *later*, most likely in 1997. No doubt, it will come true eventually. But by then, it will be totally useless to investors who relied on his first prediction and sold when they should have held.

5. They take advantage of long-term trends

Over the long term, the broad domestic markets have gone up in nearly three out of four years for at least five decades. If you always said "up" at the beginning of every year, you'd be right most of the time.

6. They keep making the same call

Since the markets keep going up and down, if you forecast either direction consistently, you're bound to be right some of the time. (Certain people who typically predict bear markets are famous for this.)

7. They lie

You may see a market timer claim to have been right "86 percent of the time over the past ten years." Eighty-six percent of what? If the timer says the market will go up, for example, what does he or she count as an "up?" The market goes up and down a little or a lot every day. Depending on how much of a move you want to count, you can easily have a "success rate" of 90 percent. The claim may be literally true in some meaningless way, but basically it's a lie.

8. All of the above

By combining these techniques, some market timers can manufacture "records" that amaze and awe the innocent. Economists remain unmoved.

Don't forget luck

Luck, as we've seen, has wide parameters. It's no big deal, for example, to get seven heads out of ten tries when you're flipping coins. Similarly, there could be a market timer who has called seven of the last ten turns in the markets. This proves nothing. There is no reason to believe his or her next ten calls will be any better than the results of random choice. Luck is always there, snickering behind the curtain.

Columnist Fred Brock reinforces this point in the December 1996 issue of *The New York Times*. Trying to be kind, he nevertheless spears the heart of year-end prognosticators:

> It's fascinating that so few stocks show up on more than one list. . . . Presumably, different stocks pickers are using different research and analytical criteria, but the average reader might be forgiven for suspecting that the experts don't have a clue.

This also applies to predictions about the markets. Some experts say they're going up; others, equally revered, say they're going down. Whom do you believe?

3. THEY HAVE HIGH COSTS

In most industries, low-cost companies drive out high-cost companies. Not so in the mutual fund industry. The December 1996 issue of *Institutional Investor* reports the following quip:

> "I think of the investment management business as being, next to the Colombian [cocaine] cartels, the most attractive marginal cost structure there is," only half jokes Jeffrey Slocum, head of the consulting firm Jeffrey Slocum & Associates.

High-margin companies survive—or even thrive—because buyers don't know how to evaluate the product (net return per unit of risk) or the impact of costs. When we discussed risk and return in chapter 4, we saw that net return can be a lot less than reported return, especially on an after-tax basis. Now we'll look at costs in greater detail.

These comments are based mainly on parts of two books: John Bogle's *Bogle on Mutual Funds* and Sheldon Jacobs's *Guide to Successful No-Load Investing,* both of which were mentioned earlier. Bogle, of course, is the champion of low-cost index funds (and low-cost funds in general). Jacobs has been a leader in promoting the advantages of no-load funds.

The ABCDs of sales charges

The better to confuse you, many fund companies offer four or more ways of paying sales charges and expenses, each referred to by a letter of the alphabet. The A shares usually hit you with an up-front load that takes a chunk out of the amount you invest. The other choices offer various ways of paying the charge over time, implying less total damage. Not so. They all attack you with the same machete. In the January 1998 issue of *Individual Investor,* author Andrew Feinberg reports:

> According to my quick-and-dirty math, after eight years you'd pay 13% in annual expenses on the A shares, plus the 5.75% up-front load, for a total of 18.75%. With the B shares, you'd pay a total of 19%.

No matter how you slice it, load funds give the investor an F. Since about 60 percent of non-index funds have a sales charge, let's look into that.

UP-FRONT SALES LOAD

Load funds charge a certain percentage to invest in their fund. Back in the fifties and early sixties, the standard charge was

8.5 percent. Investors eventually resisted this enormous hit, and the standard load was dropped to 3 to 6 percent.

The charge goes to the fund *company*, not to the fund itself. Companies use this money to compensate people who sell their funds—usually registered representatives at brokerage firms, banks, and insurance companies. As discussed earlier, a sales load has nothing to do with the performance of a fund, and there is rarely a reason to pay one. Jacobs provides extensive documentation of this point. Studies by the Wharton School of Finance and Commerce, Fund Scope, CDA/Wiesenberger, and *Consumer Reports* all show that load funds, despite superior hype, perform no better than no-loads. In fact, Jacobs cites his own study showing that no-load funds as a group have outperformed their higher-cost rivals. This supports Bogle's contention that cost is one of the prime determinants of net return in most asset classes.

This truth hurts: It's important to understand how much sales loads lower your net return. It's not, as a salesperson might say, "5 percent spread over all the years you're in the fund." It's 5 percent taken off the top, money that's not growing for you. So front-end loads hurt your return in two ways:

You lose the amount of the load itself
You lose the *return* on the load

Let's say you invest $25,000 in a 5 percent load fund. You lose $1,250 right away. Down the road, if the fund triples in value, you lose $1,250 times three, or $3,750, which is *15 percent* of your original $25,000. Ouch. As mentioned, when you see fund returns posted in publications or sales brochures, the numbers do *not* count the effect of sales loads. That's up to you to figure out by reading the fine print and doing the arithmetic.

Today, the typical load fund charges less than the original 8.5 percent. But don't feel sorry for the fund industry. Showing its usual ingenuity, it has invented other charges to make up for the drop:

THE 12B-1 FEE

This charge takes its name from a section of the Investment Company Act of 1940, which allows mutual funds to charge investors a fee to offset the cost of advertising and other forms of promotion. About 60 percent of all funds have a 12b-1 fee, which runs anywhere from .25 percent to a chilling 1 percent of assets.

For no-load funds, a 12b-1 is technically an expense, because it's part of the fund's total expense ratio. I'm covering it here because it's still one of those "charges you pay so you can be sold." And a sneaky one, at that, because many fund owners don't know they're paying it. It's buried in the expense ratio. So you really have to read the fine print to catch this one. The rationale for the charge is that fund companies have to have some way to pay their marketing costs. But that assumes you have the benefit of a knowledgeable salesperson who helps you understand what you're buying and why it's good for you. Without that kind of added value, the 12b-1 is just more money out of your pocket.

CONTINGENT DEFERRED SALES LOAD

This is one of the alphabet versions referred to earlier. The key word is *contingent*. With this kind of load, the salesperson doesn't have to ask for the commission up front. Instead, the story goes like this:

> Yes, there's a sales charge of 6 percent. But it's contingent on how long you stay in the fund. For every year you stay, the charge goes down by 1 percent. If you cash out after six years, you pay nothing.

Good try. Except for a couple of problems. First, the contingent deferred sales load is almost always accompanied by a 12b-1 fee. Like bacon and eggs, they go together. The bad part is, the 12b-1 is charged every year, so its effect keeps growing. It stays at the same percentage, but takes a larger and larger bite as your assets grow. Bogle points out that for a young person saving for retirement, it could eventually come to more than 15 percent of the amount originally invested.

LOADS ON INTEREST OR REINVESTED DIVIDENDS

A small number of funds try this gimmick. There's no up-front load, but they get you another way. The fund charges you every time it reinvests dividends from a stock fund or interest from a bond fund. Again, this practice is usually described in the fine print. And, of course, the fund's advertised return does not reflect the cost of reinvestment. Read the prospectus. You can't be too careful.

Operating expenses

In addition to sales charges, funds have "expense ratios," the fund's operating expenses expressed as a percent of total assets. These are legitimate and necessary costs—up to a point. Here's the breakdown and normal range of expenses:

Investment advisory fee:	From .5 to 1 percent
Administrative:	From .2 to .4 percent
Other operating fees:	From .1 to .3 percent

Based on the above, non-index domestic stock funds should be available with costs as low as .8 percent. In fact the average expense ratio is about 1.5 percent. The difference could represent the amount of a 12b-1 fee or other costs you have to pay.

Different kinds of funds have different cost structures. Funds that invest in foreign securities are more expensive to run than those that focus on the United States. This is especially true of emerging market funds, where the cost of research and trading is abnormally high. Expense ratios can be more than 2 percent. To a lesser extent, this is also true of domestic Small Cap funds, because it's often hard to get good data on small companies, and transaction costs are higher. *But there are limits to what you should pay.* Remember that operating expenses are a constant drag on your returns, so it pays to shop for efficient funds.

OTHER EXPENSES

You may have to pay a one-time, 1 percent charge to buy into certain funds, especially those with high costs, like emerging market funds. There may also be a 1-percent redemption charge, which is benign, *provided* it goes to the fund itself and not to the fund company. As a payment to the fund, it benefits shareholders, because it doesn't force buy-and-holders to pay the transaction costs caused by traders.

THE COST YOU DON'T HEAR ABOUT

Transaction fees are what a fund pays to buy or sell securities—brokerage commissions, plus the difference between the price asked and the price paid. You won't see these costs in sales brochures or prospectuses; they're included in the fund's reported performance. But that doesn't mean they're unimportant. In *Bogle on Mutual Funds,* Bogle figures the damage to be about 1 percent for a fund with a 75 percent turnover—the higher the turnover, the greater the damage. That 1 percent is *on top* of operating expenses. Add it all up, and you've got a hefty burden, as we're about to see.

DOES IT PAY TO WORRY ABOUT EXPENSES?

A few percent here, a few percent there—in the end, does it make any real difference? Yes. A fund's total expenses can have a major effect on a fund's return. Bogle makes this point very convincingly in his chapter on how to select a bond mutual fund. For the three-year period ended December 1992, he cites a dramatic difference in net return for bond funds:

> The lowest-cost [bond] funds outpaced the highest-cost funds by between +1.0% and +2.2% annually. The average enhancement in return was +1.8% per year.

Bogle then shows the power of that 1.8 percent advantage. Over a ten-year period, a bond fund earning 8.8 percent, instead of 7 percent, would push an original $10,000 investment from $19,700 up to $23,200, an increase of 18 percent.

The lower the return, the more important the level of costs. Simple arithmetic shows why:

1% out of a 15% return =   7% reduction in return
1% out of a 5% return =   20% reduction in return

In other words, the 1 percent charge hits you approximately three times harder with the 5 percent return than with the 15 percent return. That's why it's so important to make sure your money market and bond funds have low costs. Bogle points out that the range of money market costs extends from under .5 percent to as much as 2 percent. And many of these funds are available for around .3 percent, or less. In any event, there is no reason to pay more than .5 percent. No matter how loudly a headline shouts, simple arithmetic shouts louder.

Be careful about money market funds claiming a high return. Very often, the return comes from taking more risk or reducing the management fee for a short time, only to raise it later. Retailers call it "bait and switch."

THE CLINCHER

If you have any lingering doubts about the importance of expenses, this should dispel them: Morningstar, Inc., the Chicago fund research company, has a study in which it divides funds into five groups, based on their expense ratios. The result: There's an opposite correlation between size of expense ratio and size of return—the higher the cost, the lower the return, group by group.

A shopping guide

We've just reviewed a variety of sales charges and several kinds of expenses. You may wonder how different fund families stack up in terms of average costs. *Money* magazine answered that question in a 1992 study of the stock and bond funds in the twenty-nine largest fund companies for a three-year period. (Money market funds were excluded.) The following are annual costs:

Average of all 29 fund families:	2.2%
Highest-cost fund family:	3.5%
Lowest-cost fund family:	.4%

These figures tell us that the average annual cost of a fund in the most expensive fund family was *nine times higher* than in the least expensive fund family. It pays to shop.

4. THEY HAVE TO USE MORE JUDGMENT THAN SCIENCE

Every time a fund manager buys or sells a block of securities, he or she is making a judgment. If judgment were a good thing, you would expect funds with the highest turnover (the highest number of judgments) to have the highest return. In fact, the reverse may be true. A 1997 issue of *Bloomberg Personal* reports on the results of a Morningstar study that analyzed the performance of U.S. stock funds for one, three, five, and ten years. According to Bloomberg, the major finding was as follows:

For the one-year period ended June 30, 1997, funds whose average holding period was at least five years rose 27.1 percent, on average, while those that held their stocks one year or less gained only 17.55 percent.

5. THEY WORK IN EXTREMELY COMPETITIVE MARKETS

Picture fifty passenger cars lined up at the start of a race. They've all been adjusted to have identical performance. They're driven by drivers of near equal skill. The ground in front of each car is identical. Given those conditions, you would expect all the cars to cross the finish line at almost the same instant.

That's the general idea of what's called the "efficient market." In each asset class (or small group of asset classes), you've got hundreds or thousands of fund managers. They all study a similar universe of securities. They all work with similar information. They all get that information at about the same time. They compete by trying to be the first to recognize and act on a potentially profitable situation. For most asset classes, the result is what you would expect: It's very hard for any fund manager to stay ahead of the pack. That doesn't keep a manager from earning a profit. It just means that he or she will probably earn no more than what the markets allow for a given level of risk.

The Serengeti factor

Some asset classes can be less efficient than others. A frequently mentioned example is domestic Small Cap Stocks. There are so many of them, no manager can follow them all. And there's often a scarcity of reliable information about small companies. A hard-working fund manager with the right software screen and the drive to dig for facts has a chance to find attractive bargains.

But not for long. Picture the daily drama of Africa's Serengeti Plain. A desperate chase, a flash of fangs, and a predator makes a kill. It immediately raises its head and looks around, knowing that other predators will soon be on the scent. So will the scavengers. The predator that made the kill is lucky if it gets to eat its prize without fighting off competition. This is the world of the fund manager. Everybody on "the Street" watches everybody else. The moment it appears that a manager may be on to something—judged by a sharp increase in the price of a stock or asset class—he or she has company. The feeding frenzy continues until the price goes up so much that the stock or asset class is no longer attractive. (This also works in reverse. A whiff of selling pressure can lead to a stampede of sales.) On Wall Street as on the Serengeti, the life of an advantage may be measured in minutes.

6. THEY USE BLUNT TOOLS TO MAKE INVESTMENT DECISIONS

In their effort to predict the future and outscore their competitors, fund managers use one or both of the following:

Technical analysis
Fundamental analysis

I realize I'm getting technical again, but bear with me. The points made in this section are too important simply to assert; you need to understand what I mean by "blunt tools."

Technical analysis

Loosely, technical analysis refers to the study of past patterns of trading volume and price changes for a security, asset class, or mixture of asset classes. Technical analysts are sometimes called "chartists." They spend their time creating and looking at charts that track volume and price. You would be right to wonder why they do this. It appears that they believe their charts embody investor opinions and therefore reflect investor intentions. Or something like that. I do not pretend to have a complete understanding of their doctrine or tribal folklore.

Nearly all economists have the same opinion about technical

analysis: There's no reason it should work, and it doesn't. It's tea leaves and Tarot cards. Whenever it looks like it worked, it's just coincidence—association, not causality. Hagin reviews one study after another confirming that chart patterns are no different from random behavior:

> Several hundred tests of decision rules based on moving averages, filters, thresholds, consistently found no evidence in support of technical analysis.

A few studies have reported charting techniques that have produced statistically significant patterns. But after deductions for transaction costs, profits were no greater than those from a simple buy-and-hold strategy. In *A Random Walk Down Wall Street*, Malkiel explains *why* technical analysis doesn't work:

> First, it should be noted that the chartist buys in only after price trends have been established, and sells only after they have been broken. Since sharp reversals in the market may occur quite suddenly, the chartist will often miss the boat. . . . Second, such techniques must ultimately be self-defeating. As more and more people use it, the value of any technique depreciates.

Fundamental analysis

The vast majority of non-index fund managers use this technique, believing that it is grounded in logic and supporting data. The basic idea of fundamental analysis is to find a stock's "intrinsic" value—its "true" economic worth. If the market price is lower than the intrinsic value, the stock is ripe for purchase; if higher, it goes on the "sell" list.

Fund managers search for intrinsic value by studying fundamental data about the company and its industry. Concerning the company, managers estimate things like quality of management, earnings growth record, rank in industry, and so on. Concerning the industry, they estimate the impact of changing technology, foreign competition, and much more.

There are three basic steps in the most common form of fundamental analysis:

1. Estimate a stock's future earnings per share.
2. Estimate its future price-earnings ratio (price divided by 12-month earnings).
3. Multiply the two numbers to get the expected future value.

This process is satisfying because it yields a specific number, which creates the illusion that truth has been discovered. But often that's all it is—an illusion. Estimating future earnings per share requires judgment; so does estimating the future price-earnings ratio. And judgment is fallible. Multiplying two "not sures" by each other does not give you a "definite." It gives you a guess in numerical form. Another problem is the length of time the manager chooses for his or her predictions. As Malkiel points out, it adds another loose end to an already loose process:

> There is always some combination of growth rate and growth period that will produce any specific price. In this sense, it is intrinsically impossible, given human nature, to calculate the intrinsic value of a share.

Without a reliable value for "intrinsic value," the whole edifice of fundamental analysis stands on sand. It's true there are many times when a price (or price range) predicted by fundamental analysis proves to be accurate. This can occur when nothing unforeseen happens in the economy, the markets, the industry, or the company—a highly unlikely situation. You can see the result of all this when you read the financial press:

The Great Predictors don't agree with each other.

They have widely different methods for picking stocks, for example. Publications tend to describe a particular method with awed admiration, as though it were the only way to manage a fund. Then, without cracking a smile, they may be equally lavish in describing an *opposing* method—in the same issue. Makes you wonder.

7. THEY COMPETE IN A ZERO-SUM GAME

This is pure logic. A zero-sum game is one in which every point won is offset by an equal number of points lost. Poker is a zero-sum game—all the winnings come out of the losers' pockets. The world of non-index funds is similar when it comes to outperforming a market average. The moment a fund performs well enough to beat the average, another fund (which was formerly *above* average) must fall *below* average.

Non-index fund management is a dead-serious game precisely because one manager's success can mean another manager's failure. In an article in the fall 1994 issue of *The Journal of Portfolio Management*, Keith Ambachtsheer pictures the markets as a battleground:

> Reality is that, as long as trading continues to be dominated by active managers, financial markets are profoundly adversarial. . . . Obviously, if you want to buy a block at a certain price, and the other party is prepared to sell it to you at that price, it can't be a good deal for both of you.

The article is addressed to fund managers and plan sponsors. But it highlights a point average investors need to consider: You may have, in your opinion, an absolutely brilliant non-index fund manager with an outstanding track record. You may have faith in his or her ability to beat the average performance of a given asset class. But it isn't just a faceless abstraction that your manager has to beat; it's all the other brilliant managers who are doing their brilliant best to beat *your* brilliant manager.

8. THEY MAY BE OVERWHELMED BY CASH INFLOW

As Malkiel explained in his introduction, the size of a non-index fund can affect its performance. This is especially true when there's a sudden increase in size. A fund manager with a good track record may be deluged with cash inflow from ever-hopeful investors. He or she now has to find a lot of good buys, instead of just a few. This can be a serious problem, as *The New York Times* pointed out in an article entitled "A Startling Discovery at a Dreyfus Fund," in a December 1996 business section. The article begins by reporting that the Dreyfus Aggressive Growth fund grew 82 percent in the year ended September 30, "more than any other mutual fund in the country." Yet, according to the article, investors in the fund *lost* $31 million as of the date of publication. The *Times* explains how this occurred: "The simple explanation for that seemingly impossible feat is that the fund's early gains were more than wiped out by declines after the fund attracted a great deal of money." This is one more example of why you can't trust the published returns of non-index funds.

9. THEY HAVE TO HOLD CASH

As we've seen, non-index funds keep some of their investors' assets in money market securities, which the fund industry calls "cash." The amount depends on the individual fund, but generally runs from 5 percent to 15 percent, with the average at about 9 percent. Non-index managers do this on a continuing basis to be ready for investor withdrawals. They may also do it when they think the markets are headed south. In any case, holding cash is a drag on performance. The history of the stock market shows that most of its upward movement happens in short bursts. If you miss out on one of them, it can significantly lower your long-term gains. That's why a simple "buy-and-hold" strategy tends to beat every other approach.

10. THEY MAY INVEST IN UNFAMILIAR ASSET CLASSES

I'm referring to style drift, which we discussed earlier. Competitive pressure often drives non-index fund managers to get performance any way they can, which may mean going outside their announced asset class. This creates two problems: When managers leave their asset class, they often move into higher-risk securities, in hopes of earning higher returns. But higher risk means higher volatility.

The second problem is also one we've seen before: Nobody's good at everything. Managers who specialize in large-cap stocks, for example, may find themselves in strange waters when they venture into the world of small-cap stocks.

SUMMARY

We've just examined ten reasons why most non-index fund managers haven't been able to keep up with their relevant index:

1. They have to make predictions.
2. They can't time the markets.
3. They have high costs.
4. They have to use more judgment than science.
5. They work in extremely competitive markets.
6. They use blunt tools to make investment decisions.

7. They compete in a zero-sum game.
8. They may be overwhelmed by cash inflows from investors.
9. They have to hold cash.
10. They may invest in unfamiliar asset classes.

And don't forget the all-too-familiar situation created when the presiding Great Predictor leaves his or her fund. (The average tenure of a fund manager is less than four years.) Do you stay with the fund? Or do you follow the manager? Index funds avoid all these problems. Sometimes, life can be simple.

THE NEW WISDOM

All this adds up to a flat-out denial of the old wisdom about the way average people should invest—buy individual stocks and bonds or individual non-index funds. The new wisdom says:

Avoid or minimize stocks, bonds, and non-index funds. Don't expect a fund to be good in the future because it was good in the past. Put all or most of your money into a diversified portfolio of index funds, balanced to fit your situation.

The new wisdom is not just an alternative; it shoves the old wisdom aside and stands in its place. The new wisdom is not based on my opinion, nor on the opinion of investment gurus. It's based on hard data—gathered, analyzed, and reported by mutual fund research firms and prominent economists.

CHAPTER 8

A Noble Invention

THE FIRST THING TO UNDERSTAND IS THAT AN INVESTMENT portfolio functions like a football team. Each component has a different job to do, and success depends more on how well the parts work together than on the excellence of any single part.

The information on portfolios in this chapter is not supposed to be in a book written mainly for unsophisticated investors. It's considered too technical. But I'm no technical whiz, and I can understand it, at least in principle. And if I can, you can. You may ask, "Why bother?" The answer is simple. This information will help you make more money than you would without it. Specifically, you'll see how to earn the highest return for a given level of risk.

THE 92 PERCENT SOLUTION

What would you expect to learn if you examined the performance of large pension plans? These are *defined benefit* plans, in which the employer—the "plan sponsor"—puts up all the money and manages the plan as it sees fit. What you've got here is professional investment people hiring and supervising professional money managers. Experts leading experts. If there is any place where expert judgment should make a big difference, this must be it.

This hypothesis was put to the test by Gary Brinson and colleagues and reported in the May 1991 issue of *Financial Analysts Journal*. The major finding was a shocker:

> Active investment decisions by plan sponsors and managers did little on average to improve performance over the 10-year period, December 1977 to December 1987. . . . Specifically, data from 82 large pension plans indicate that investment policy explained, on average, 91.5 percent of the variation in quarterly total plan returns.

According to this study, the plan sponsors and money managers contributed only 8.5 percent to total return. To understand this result, let's back up a little. Major plan sponsors typically have an "investment policy," a baseline portfolio that allocates a specified percent of assets to a variety of asset classes. In theory, this is a starting point for clever money managers who are supposed to improve on the return of the baseline portfolio. In this study, the clever money managers, working with the plan sponsors, did very little. The unadorned, unmanaged asset classes—in effect, index funds—contributed almost 92 percent.

This does not mean every similar study would come up with the same percentage. It's a rough idea of what tends to happen.

Still, why such a dramatic result? *The answer is portfolio power.*

Up until now, we've been talking about index funds versus non-index funds, always with the idea of comparing funds in the same asset class. This is different. Now we're talking about the return on a *blend* of funds—a *portfolio*. More formally, an investment portfolio can be defined as a combination of different kinds of investments, structured to meet an investor's goals for risk, return, and time period. For most people, the investments are stocks, bonds, or mutual funds. Every investor should have a balanced portfolio in some form. You'll see why as we move along.

CONCENTRATION VERSUS DIVERSIFICATION

Building a portfolio implies diversifying your assets, which brings up a basic point. There are at least two different investment philosophies: concentration and diversification. Concentration means owning a small group of *similar* securities or funds. It implies an ability to predict the future, because you're buying a group of investments that tend to behave in a similar way. If you're right, you win big; if you're wrong, you lose big.

Diversification, on the other hand, means owning a relatively large group of *dissimilar* securities or funds. It implies that the investor knows he or she can't predict the future and has therefore prepared for a variety of futures. The philosophy you choose depends on your capacity to accept the results of risk.

The case against concentration became clear during the sixties and seventies, as study after study came to the same conclusion: Technical analysis doesn't work, and fundamental analysis works poorly. Security analysts and fund managers could not, in fact, reliably predict the future price of selected securities. *Without that ability, concentration makes little sense,* because there's no dependable way to decide which securities to concentrate on. A high-profile example is the rise and fall of "glamour stocks" in the sixties.

Stock-picking geniuses concentrated on a small number of stocks in a narrow range of industries. Their efforts attracted so much attention (and money) that their predictions became self-fulfilling—the stocks went up because the geniuses said they would, and everybody rushed to get in on the action.

More recently, in the mid-nineties, some pundits have advocated buying stocks of a few giant companies and changing them once a year—extreme concentration. They say this method has an impressive twenty-year record. By now, you probably have an idea of what the flaws are. First, the advocates of this method do not show the results of *rolling* twenty-year periods. So they could have picked a particular twenty-year period when their method seemed to work, avoiding periods when it did not work.

For example, boasting a great track record, certain stocks in the Dow Industrials ("Dogs of the Dow") were sold in groups called "unit investments trusts." In the latter part of the nineties, they did poorly—considerably worse than the S&P 500. Another daydream shattered.

Suppose the Dogs of the Dow method were actually valid. What would happen? As these stocks prospered, fund managers would notice. They would quickly run the stocks through their computers to learn on what basis the stocks were selected. Then they would "back-test" the method—study how it worked in the past. If the back-test looked promising, they would buy the stocks. If this approach produced above-average gains, packs of predators would pounce on it, quickly driving up the price of the selected stocks. Then it wouldn't work anymore, because the buy-in price would be too high. The few fund managers who got in early would do well; the rest would not.

And so it goes. You can argue that *your* fund manager will be among the early arrivals who earn above-average gains. The odds are against it. There are hundreds of methods out there. Most of them don't work. The few that do are quickly priced out of operation by the process just described. As Rodney Alldredge of Daniels and Alldredge Investment Management in Birmingham, Alabama, has pointed out, this scenario can go a step further. Once you have an objective criteria for selecting stocks, you can create an index, then an index fund, which, because of its low costs and low turnover, will probably do better than the average non-index manager who tries to follow the formula.

Getting back to the glamour stocks of the sixties, you don't have to be a genius to see that the glamour-stock approach was a thin thread from which to hang the weight of a market. Sure enough, the thread snapped, and the glamour stocks came crashing down, splintering reputations in the process.

After that (no surprise), people became more interested in diversification. It was not a new idea, but it contrasted appealingly with the downdraft produced by concentration. The basic idea was simple: If you bought a lot of different securities, you reduced your total risk—you weren't putting all your eggs in one basket.

As originally conceived, though, diversification meant owning someone's perception of the best stocks in a broad range of industries, either in a mutual fund or on your own. (If you wanted to be conservative, you also put some money in bonds.) Mutual fund salespeople pushed this idea, pointing out that very few people were rich enough to own dozens of stocks and bonds. Millions of people were impressed with that argument, and sales of mutual funds began to take off. This was the "old diversification." It simply meant owning parts of many companies in a variety of industries. Nothing more complicated than that. Meanwhile, a process had started that would give diversification a precise new meaning.

THE BIRTH OF
PORTFOLIO THINKING

The year is 1952. An unknown graduate student named Harry Markowitz presents his humble self to Professors Milton Friedman and Jacob Marschak to get their reaction to his doctoral dissertation on portfolio theory. Friedman tells him his paper is valid, but he doesn't look happy. "Harry," he says, "You have a problem. [This paper] is not Economics; it's not Business Administration; it's not Mathematics." Professor Marschak adds, "And it's not Literature." Friedman concludes, "We cannot award you a Ph.D. in economics for a dissertation that is not economics." They send Markowitz out into the hall so they can confer. You can imagine his state of mind. A doctoral candidate's dissertation represents a large part of the candidate's past and an even larger part of his or her future. After a five-minute wait, Marschak comes out and says, "Congratulations, Doctor Markowitz." Evidently, the professors felt that Markowitz was on to something big. (This anecdote comes from the back pages of Harry Markowitz's highly influential book *Portfolio Selection*, Blackwell Publishers, 1995 printing.)

Soon after this incident, Markowitz's paper appeared in *The Journal of Finance*. It hardly made a ripple. But thirty-eight years later, he shared the Nobel Prize in economics for what is now called modern portfolio theory (MPT). William Sharpe, whom we met in chapter 4, and Merton Miller received the Nobel Prize at the same time for their own contributions to MPT. Today, it's a virtual religion in the professional investment community. Hundreds of billions of dollars are invested according to its principles, which argues for MPT being one of the great inventions of the twentieth century.

Markowitz started with a disarmingly simple observation: *Investors don't just want to maximize return; they want to maximize return while minimizing risk.* I would guess that some of his earliest readers responded with something like, "So, what else is new? Sure, that's what they want. But return is proportional to risk. You can't have one without the other."

In effect, Markowitz responded, "True, but I think there's a way to give investors the best of both worlds—maximum return for a given level of risk, or the reverse—minimum risk for a given level of return." His method of doing that was based on another simple observation: *Different stocks and bonds tend to respond differently to the same events in the economy or in the securities markets.* This is also true of asset classes. A change in interest rates, for example, can drive some asset classes up and others down. Again, this was not news. On the surface, it sounded like the well-known fact that diversification reduces risk. But Markowitz, more than anyone else at the time, understood the implications: When you have a portfolio of stocks or funds that move in different ways, you have an opportunity to go beyond the usual benefits of diversification. Specifically:

> You can minimize risk for a given level of return (or maximize return for given level of risk) by (1) selecting portfolio components that tend to behave very differently from each other in their response to the same economic or market events, and (2) mathematically optimizing the percentage of each component in the portfolio.

I know I'm getting technical again, but hang in there. This is a Big Idea, not just in the academic world, but also in your personal financial world. Diversifying according to the principles of MPT, versus the old way, could enlarge your nest egg by many thousands of dollars—a large enough difference to change the college you can afford for your children, or the kind of lifestyle you can lead when you retire.

Let's look at a hypothetical example to explain a basic principle of MPT. Say you own stock in a fast-food chain. When unemployment is over 6 percent, people get serious about cutting expenses. Business is good and profits go up. The stock price rises enough to deliver a total return of 30 percent. But when unemployment falls *below* 6 percent, people prefer to eat in fancier places. Business for your low-end chain drops off. Profits go down, depressing the price of the stock. Return falls to a *minus* 10 percent. Your total return over time is the average of both situations—10 percent. (Assume that unemployment is above 6 percent half the time and below 6 percent the other half.)

You put up with this for awhile, but it worries you. Suppose an emergency comes along, and you have to sell the stock when it's down. You'll lose money—not a happy prospect. But then you have an idea: "Suppose I also invest in a certain *high-end* chain of restaurants. My estimates show that I'll have a stock that does the exact opposite of my first stock. If I put an equal amount of money in both, I'll have the best of both worlds."

Sure enough, the new stock delivers a 30 percent return when unemployment drops below 6 percent and minus 10 percent when unemployment is above 6 percent. The total picture looks like this:

	UNEMPLOYMENT		VOLATILITY (RANGE OF RETURNS)	AVERAGE RETURN
	BELOW 6%	ABOVE 6%		
Low-end stock return	30%	-10%	40%	10%
High-end stock return	-10%	30%	40%	10%
Portfolio return	10%	10%	0%	10%

Congratulations. You now have a miniportfolio that eliminates the volatility caused by the level of unemployment. At the same time, you've kept your average return at 10 percent. You achieved this result by buying investments that move in opposite directions to the same extent. A similar scenario could be constructed that would show how to increase your return while keeping the original risk level. Think of this idea as the "piston effect." The pistons in your car's engine go up and down at different times, but the motor runs evenly.

A COUNTERINTUITIVE RESULT

In real stock and bond markets, things don't work out that neatly. There aren't many portfolio components that reliably move in opposite directions. What you tend to have is stocks, bonds, and asset classes that move in the same direction, but at different rates or to different degrees. A short-term drop in interest rates, for example, might tend to help Small Cap stocks more than Large Cap stocks: Smaller companies tend to raise more of their capital by short-term borrowing than do large companies.

All of which brings up the subject of "correlation," which can be described as the extent to which two different types of investments tend to move up and down together. It's one of the key ideas of MPT:

> The lower the correlation among different components of a portfolio, the higher the benefits of diversification.

That's over-simplified for brevity, but the basic idea is correct. In your investment portfolio—at work or on your own—you want funds that have the lowest possible correlation with each other, because that will give you the most diversification and the least portfolio risk for a given level of return. This idea is so powerful that it produces a counterintuitive result. You would think that if you add a high-risk fund to your portfolio, you would increase its total risk. Not necessarily, as Markowitz points out in *Portfolio Selection:*

> The addition of the risky security [in this example] produces a more conservative portfolio than the addition of the conservative security. This illustrates a basic principle: the security which is risky or conservative, appropriate or inappropriate, for one portfolio may be the opposite for another. One must think of selecting a portfolio as a whole, not securities per se.

This principle also applies to index funds: Choose your funds not just for their stand-alone merits, but also for how they affect your total portfolio.

REDUCING RISKS

For a better understanding of diversification, let's take another look at risk. In this context, you can think of risk as coming in two flavors:

1. *Asset class risk:* The price of a security or fund can move up and down because of changes in the price of its asset class. If most energy stocks make a move, for example, it will probably affect *all* stocks and funds in the energy group.
2. *Component risk:* A security or non-index fund can have its own price movement, independent of its asset class. If a company reports a big, unexpected loss, its stock will probably fall in price even if its asset class goes up.

These two kinds of risk, taken together, make up the total risk of a stock, bond, or fund. Diversification, as redefined by Markowitz, all but eliminates component risk for individual stocks, bonds, and non-index funds. On average, in a well-diversified portfolio, any price change in one security tends to be offset by an opposite price change in another.

Of course, you can also eliminate component risk with an index fund, because an index fund *is* the asset class (or very nearly). But here we're talking about combining a *variety of funds* into a single portfolio—a single team. *In that case, the individual funds take the place of stocks and bonds, and the principles of MPT apply to the funds.* This is a major point. It means that you can use MPT techniques to reduce asset class risk, just as you use MPT to reduce the component risk associated with individual securities.

For example, real estate investment trust funds tend to have a low correlation with Large Cap growth funds, and emerging market funds may have a low correlation with both. Each of the three funds has its own unique response to economic and market events. Put the three together, and you're beginning to use MPT in a highly effective way.

PARTIAL VERSUS FULL DIVERSIFICATION

Contrast that structure with the implied strategy of an investor who thinks he or she can diversify by buying, for example, three Large Cap funds and an equity income fund. "I must be diversified," the investor thinks. "I own part of hundreds of different companies, and I own different types of funds." This is a dangerous half-truth. The investor is diversified when it comes to individual securities, *but not in regard to asset classes*. Most equity income funds consist of stocks from large companies. So what this investor owns is a concentration of Large Cap stocks—with all the inherent risks and potential rewards of concentration. Markowitz sums it up succinctly:

> One hundred securities whose returns rise and fall in near unison afford little more protection than the uncertain return of a single security.

FORECASTS, NOT PREDICTIONS

Because of MPT's inherent design, experts can use it to forecast, not near-term prices, but long-term, risk-return relationships. People who know how to use MPT can say, "There are no guarantees, but long term, if you take this much risk, in this kind of portfolio, it would be reasonable to anticipate this much return." How is that possible?

The short answer is that it took three Nobel Prize winners and some very fancy math. More specifically, you can say things about a mathematically designed group such as a portfolio that you cannot say about a single component, such as a stock or even a mutual fund. Life insurance companies, for example, are able to quote exact rates, even though they don't know how long any individual person might live. They have an excellent idea, though, about how long the entire group of insured people will live. A properly designed investment portfolio provides a somewhat similar advantage.

Caution: Output depends on input. To apply MPT, you need to feed certain data into the formulas, especially expected return, a measure of volatility, and the correlation between each pair of funds. The first two items could involve a limited degree of judgment, and to that extent, the results of an MPT analysis could be wrong. If the portfolio builder avoids judgment and uses only very long-term historical data, there is still a chance of error. A rolling, fifty-year record of risk and return is generally thought to be more reliable than using only the last ten years. But even in this case, past may not be prologue.

Recognizing those reservations, a long-term forecast about risk-return relationships is very different from predicting the price of a stock or bond. For one thing, it's more reliable, partly because of another observation that Markowitz made: The seventy-year record of stock and bond prices reveals that, although returns have jumped around unpredictably, the *relationship* between level of risk and level of return has remained remarkably consistent. This fact, coupled with taking advantage of the differing behavior of portfolio components, allows MPT practitioners to make useful forecasts about risk-return relationships. The fruits of their labors—well, part of it, anyway—can be represented in a graph (see page 148).

The vertical line represents an increasing amount of return; the horizontal line shows an increasing amount of risk (volatility). The Best Deal line, therefore, shows a range of optimal risk-return relationships for any mix of portfolio components.

Ideally, you want your portfolio to be on the Best Deal line,

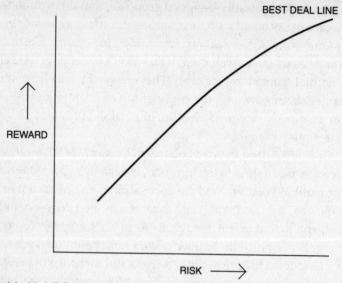

Graph by Mark E. Evans.

because that line defines the most efficient combinations of asset classes. *Exception:* If your situation calls for low risk—for example, if you are retired—it may be wise to drop below the Best Deal line and accept a less-efficient portfolio in return for less volatility.

The graph on page 149 shows the situation of two investors: Steve, who is sixty-two, and Leslie, thirty-two. The main thing on Steve's mind is not to lose capital when the markets go down. So he wants to keep his risk at a low level. Leslie isn't worried about down markets. She's young enough to see them through and be there when the bulls come back. The Best Deal lines show Markowitz's original idea at work: Both Steve and Leslie get what they want, and they get it with a risk-return relationship that has been mathematically optimized.

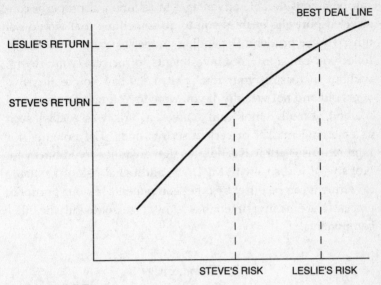

Graph by Mark E. Evans.

THREE ADVANTAGES

The eminent economist Milton Friedman is famous for pointing out that there is no free lunch (yes, the same Milton Friedman who approved Markowitz's dissertation). In this context, it means you have to give up something when you invest with a diversified portfolio. You can no longer bet all your money on a potential star performer—stock or mutual fund—and hope to make a killing. The more you diversify, the more you tend to approach an average return. On the other hand, if you invest with a portfolio built according to MPT principles—and build that portfolio with index funds—you will gain at least three advantages:

1. The MPT edge

As explained, a portfolio that follows MPT principles is designed to provide the most return for a given level of risk. That, by itself, can be a considerable advantage. In addition, a properly constructed portfolio enables you to do something that would not otherwise be prudent: Depending on the structure of your portfolio, you can add risky investments to increase your return, without increasing your total risk. Let's say you're fifty-five years old and not wealthy. If you were investing by a piecemeal method, you might not want to invest in a risky asset class, such as emerging market or certain sector funds. The potential for high returns is attractive, but the high volatility could hurt you. Not so—or less so—with MPT. The additional risk of a volatile investment can be offset by other components in your portfolio, *provided* the new investment has a low correlation with the other components.

2. *The index edge*

As we've seen, each asset class in your portfolio is likely, long term, to outperform the average non-index stock or bond fund in that class.

3. *Peace of mind*

Within each asset class, index funds will protect you from manager risk. Beyond that, a well-balanced portfolio gives you an investment vehicle you can live with. Assuming that long-term risk-return relationships continue, an MPT portfolio is somewhere near the best arrangement of your assets to fit your long-term needs. You don't have to go through a crisis of confidence every time something happens in the markets or the economy. Of course, you may want to rebalance your portfolio when price changes cause a significant change in the relative weighting of the asset classes in your portfolio. But the point of that effort is simply to maintain the original weighting of asset classes.

FROM THEORY TO PRACTICE

In his new book *Global Bargain Hunting: Investment Opportunities in Emerging Markets* (Simon & Schuster, 1998), Burton Malkiel shows how to apply MPT to make more money. One example: adding "EAFE" (Europe, Australasia, Far East) stocks to a portfolio. He explains a graph showing what happens to risk and return under different combinations of domestic and foreign stocks:

> Note that as the portfolio shifts from a 100 percent domestic allocation to one with gradual additions of foreign stocks, the return tends to increase because EAFE stocks produced a higher return than domestic stocks over this eleven-year period [ending 1995]. The significant point, however, is that adding some of these riskier securities actually increased the portfolio's safety level—at least for awhile.

Malkiel then makes a case for emerging market stocks. He points out that their correlation is generally very low not only with U.S. markets, but also with those of European and Asian markets in developed countries. He says:

> Over an 11-year period ending in 1995, the mix that provided the highest return available with the least risk was 61% U.S. stocks, 26% EAFE stocks, and 13% emerging market stocks.

Of course, we have to remind ourselves that the past does not predict. Take 1997, for example. Some Latin American emerging markets produced roaring returns—double those of the Dow Jones Industrial Average. In the same year, certain Asian markets fell by 50 percent or more. In the short run, a major event with global repercussions (like the deflationary effect of Asian currency devaluations) could cause asset class correlations to rise. In the long run, though, regression to mean is likely to pull correlations back to traditional levels.

HOW TO BUILD
AN MPT PORTFOLIO

At this point, you may be thinking, "Fine. But how do I build my own MPT portfolio?" The easiest way is simply to look at the final chapter, where Malkiel spells out age-related portfolios. Both the asset classes and the percentage allocations are chosen to reflect Modern Portfolio Theory.

On the other hand, you don't need mathematical precision to apply the principles of MPT. A big step forward is simply to avoid the fallacy of thinking that a variety of funds in the same asset class gives you meaningful diversification. Instead, buy index funds (or mostly index funds) in a *broad variety of asset classes*, including emerging markets and REITs (real estate investment trusts), both of which have low correlations with large-cap U.S. stock funds, which may form the bulk of your portfolio. This alone will give you constructive diversification.

SUMMARY

- Long term, about 90 percent of your portfolio return may come from the way you allocate your money among the major asset classes: stocks, bonds, and cash.
- Modern Portfolio Theory (MPT) describes how to achieve a powerful form of investment diversification: Own asset classes that behave differently in response to the same economic and market events. MPT allows you to optimize the percentage of these selected asset classes.

- A portfolio based on MPT principles is efficient. It delivers the highest estimated return for a given level of risk—or the minimum estimated risk for a given level of return.
- Avoid buying funds (index or non-index) just because they sound good individually. Evaluate each fund in terms of how closely it correlates with the rest of your portfolio. Low correlation gives you a more efficient portfolio than high correlation.
- Emerging market and REIT (Real Estate Investment Trusts) funds generally have low correlations with Large Cap domestic stock funds and offer the potential for high return—an excellent example of applying MPT principles to strengthen your portfolio.
- To build your own MPT portfolio, see the final chapter, where Malkiel discusses age-related asset allocations.

BEFORE WE MOVE ON

Time to consolidate our gains. Here are some of the main things we've learned in Part 1 of this book:

- Non-index fund managers face many formidable obstacles, including high costs, intense competition, the failure of technical analysis, and the weakness of fundamental analysis.
- In both the short and long term, stock and bond index funds have outperformed the average, relevant non-index fund over a wide range of asset classes.
- The long-term superior performance of index funds is likely to continue because of inherent advantages, including lower costs, the ability to stay fully invested, the absence of manager risk, and the tax advantage of lower capital gains distributions.
- The only purpose of a non-index fund is to outperform a relevant index fund.

- Despite some evidence of short-term price persistence, there's no practical way for average investors to select top-performing non-index funds by looking at past performance.
- Investors should not take published non-index fund performance at face value; data from these funds can mislead investors in many ways.
- The new wisdom calls for long-term investing with a diversified portfolio composed mainly or entirely of index funds, balanced to fit an investor's individual situation.
- Investors can lower risk for a given level of return (or raise return for a given level of risk) by choosing funds that have a low correlation with each other (respond differently to the same economic or market events).

Now that you know all that, how do you turn your knowledge into wealth—*more* wealth than you might have had before you picked up this book? Part 2 provides the answer.

The Five Giant Steps to Wealth

We're now ready to explore a reliable way to accumulate wealth. It's not a complex software program. It's not a formula for picking hot stocks. And you don't have to be a financial expert to understand it. The basic ideas are simple:

1. **Get a personal financial plan** (mainly, a set of goals stated in dollar amounts).
2. **Get a personal investment plan** (a strategy to reach your goal).
3. **Invest with a diversified portfolio of index funds, balanced to fit your needs** (the way to implement your strategy).
4. **Gain the maximum benefit from tax laws.**
5. **Don't try to time the markets—buy and hold, starting as soon as possible.**

That's it—the essence of successful long-term investing—and the single, most important set of ideas in this book. If you can grasp these five points and carry them out, you *will be* a successful, long-term investor.

That doesn't mean you'll have all ups and no downs. There

have been bear markets in the past; there will be bear markets in the future. It *does* mean you will progress toward your goals with a high degree of reliability. You will not be dependent on the evanescent insights of Great Predictors. You will not be dependent on luck or technical knowledge of the markets. You will have a program that works through thick and thin.

CHAPTER 9

Giant Steps 1 and 2:
Planning

PROGRAMS START WITH PLANNING; INVESTING FOR YOUR FUTURE
is no exception. We'll look at financial planning (Giant Step 1)
and investment planning (Giant Step 2) in a few minutes. But
first, some useful background:

WHAT DRIVES THE MARKETS?

You can think of the stock and bond markets as a vast playing
field where participants (people or companies) put money behind their opinions—and everyone else in the game decides if
these opinions are right or wrong. The challenge is not to find
good value, but rather to predict what *others* will see as good
value. Behind all this are several elemental forces.

"Greed and Fear. Good morning!"

I almost expect to hear that when I call a Wall Street firm. Strip away the fancy talk, and you'll find the markets tend to be driven by greed and fear. Which is why they often go too far in one direction, then too far in the other. In between, there's a band of changing width where reason rules. Emotions own the rest. This is one of the main reasons that no one can reliably predict future security prices. Market timers proclaim lofty arguments why the markets will do this or that, then cringe as greed and fear prove them wrong.

Asset class rotation

The constant interplay between greed and fear forms a backdrop for a behavior pattern called "asset class rotation." This is a central idea in portfolio building. Different asset classes take turns at the top, middle, and bottom of investor preference. There are at least three reasons for this:

1. *Economic events.* For example, a sharp rise in the value of the dollar in relation to foreign currencies will help some asset classes and hurt others.
2. *Market events.* Stock prices in a given asset class may sink to near-term lows, thereby making that class seem like a bargain.
3. *Fashion events.* There are fads in the markets just as there are in other human activities. Great Predictors support their preferences with cogent-sounding arguments, but the truth, often enough, is like taste in art: They simply know what they like.

EXTENDED EXAMPLE

Assume security analysts forecast a sharp rise in earnings for Large Cap Growth companies. The asset class rises in price. Then greed takes over, as more and more investors rush to get in on the action. The price goes way up. Eventually, at some indeterminate point, this process makes Large Cap Growth stocks seem less attractive; investors start to think of them as overpriced. The asset class hangs there for awhile, precariously balanced between greed and fear. At some point, changes in the economy set off a scare. It may be groundless, but never mind. Fear takes over. Large Cap Growth stocks plunge in price, and another asset class takes its place as king of the hill.

That's asset class rotation (sometimes called "sector" rotation). Among other things, it helps to explain why buy-and-hold almost always beats market timing as a long-term investment strategy. Great Predictors tend to stay in the overpriced asset class too long, or get out too early, or misidentify the next top-performing asset class. Meanwhile, the humble buy-and-holder just sits there with a diversified portfolio, never making news, but steadily making money.

STATISTICAL EXAMPLE

The March 9, 1997, issue of *The New York Times* reports on part of a study done by Morningstar, Inc., the Chicago fund researchers:

> In comparing returns each year for the next one, two and three years, the three *least* popular equity fund categories beat the three *most* popular categories 22 times out of 24.

Popularity was measured by net cash inflow. *Caution: Don't take this as a "sure bet" formula for making money in the stock markets. In another time period, it may not work. It's just a real-world example of asset class rotation—and the value of owning different types of index funds.

Regression to mean

As asset class rotation grabs the headlines, something else may be going on. Economists call it "regression to mean" (return to average). The term refers to the tendency of all asset classes to revert to their long-term standards of valuation. By "standards," I mean ratios like price to earnings, price to dividend, and price to book value. Think of this process as a rubber band. The more you stretch it, the more the band strains to return to its normal state. When it does (or when it overreacts), you have what's called a "market correction," or, in a more severe form, a bear market.

This is the rational part of market psychology, the part where intense competition among professional investors drives prices to a level where a stock's perceived return potential is neatly balanced by its perceived risk. This is the so-called "efficient market," where nobody gets ahead of anybody else by much, for long.

Cross currents

Every now and then, a fundamental change occurs that may alter the standards. Possible example: The seventy-three-year return on the S&P 500 has been about 11 percent. But over the past fifteen years, the return has been over 18 percent—63 percent higher. Should we change the standards of valuation for big stocks? Are big U.S. stocks worth more than before, because they're going to return more than before? Or will a bear market pull the average down to where it has been for over seven decades? Nobody knows.

The markets are like a river of roaring white water, with greed and fear pushing the markets to extremes, while the reverse current of regression to mean pushes prices toward the eddy of long-term average. And flowing under it all, there could be the subtle, but powerful force of fundamental change. When you're out on that river, you need a map (your financial and investment plans) and the right kind of craft (a portfolio that follows your plans).

GIANT STEP 1:
GET A PERSONAL FINANCIAL PLAN

Managing your financial future is like a lot of other things in life: If you know where you're going, you're more likely to get there. Many people work toward a financial goal thinking, "I'll save as much as I can. I can't do more than that." Yes, you can. You can specify goals and methods, in dollar amounts, as part of an overall plan.

This process focuses your thinking and provides a savings and investment discipline you might not otherwise have. Equally important, it provides a basis for taking specific actions to achieve quantified goals. A retirement-oriented plan, for example, could put you in a position to say something like this:

> Our target amount is (goal in dollars). To reach it, we need to invest at least $400 a month for the next fifteen years at an annual average return of 9 percent. Judging by long-term market data, this suggests we should have 70 percent of our money in stock funds, 25 percent in bond funds, and 5 percent in cash equivalents.

This statement doesn't mention life insurance, real estate, or other issues, but they can all be woven into a basic retirement plan. With that in place, you can then move on to specifying the components of your portfolio.

One of the main benefits of planning is that it will bring up issues you may have never thought about, such as: how all your assets can work together, or the best way to handle a home mortgage, or how to minimize capital gains taxes. I can't overemphasize the importance of having this kind of information. It can make the difference between getting where you need to go and running aground. *Important:* These principles and ideas also apply to your 401(k) and other kinds of tax-advantaged plans (with the exception that minimizing taxes may be less of an issue).

A financial plan integrates all pertinent information about your current and expected financial situation. In its broadest form, it answers questions like these:

- What is the total dollar amount I should aim for?
- Considering taxes, how much am I likely to earn from income sources I already have or expect to have?
- How large is the gap between the target amount and what my current sources will generate?
- How much do I need to invest per month to fill the gap?
- What role should other assets, such as life insurance and home ownership, play in the total plan?
- When investing, what risk level should I accept?

Financial plans usually focus on retirement, but they don't have to. Young people, for example, may want a plan to help them buy a home or business in the not-so-distant future. Parents may be looking for ways to accumulate money for college expenses. Planning is vital for all these goals.

Financial plans vary greatly in cost, degree of personalization, and how much they include. A plan can be as short as a couple of pages. It will suggest what your goal should be in total dollars, how much income that should generate, and how much you need to invest per month, depending on a range of estimated returns. Some comprehensive plans, on the other hand, may cover dozens of topics and run to twenty pages or more.

Three different attitudes

In this and the next two chapters, we'll review a variety of options for financial and investment planning. As we work through these options, there are a few things to keep in mind. To start, one size does not fit all. The planning source that's best for one person may not be appropriate for another. Planning depends on several factors, one of which is the amount of money you have to invest. If it's $500,000, you have a broader range of choices than someone with $50,000. Perhaps more to the point is how much you're willing to wrestle with data and investment issues. Some people like to think about investing; others find it overwhelming. To help you choose among the various options, I've arbitrarily divided people into three degrees of willingness to deal with investment issues:

1. Do *None* of It Myself
   This is someone who simply doesn't want to think about investing or doesn't have the time. The goal here is to delegate almost every aspect of the work to someone else.
2. Do *Some* of It Myself
   Here's a person who's willing to deal with investment issues and evaluate the work of others—but does not want to do much of the work. He or she is willing, however, to assemble major parts of a portfolio.
3. Do *All* of It Myself
   This investor likes the process of investing, feels comfortable with the issues, and is willing to spend the necessary time. He or she wants nothing more than useful information and tools to simplify calculations.

It would be helpful to decide whether you're in the "none," "some," or "all" category. Keep in mind there's a price to pay for avoiding work. All-of-it-myself people can get their plans free. None-of-it-myself people may have to pay a substantial amount in fees or commissions.

Finally, there are three kinds of planning: financial, investment, and estate. For convenience, people often use the single term *financial planning* to refer to all three.

How to get a financial plan

You have a choice, depending on your willingness and ability to deal with investment issues. Somewhat arbitrarily, we can say there are three ways to get a financial plan:

In person:	Mostly for none-of-it-myself people.
Over the phone:	For almost anyone.
On your own:	Mostly for all-of-it-myself people.

There are no rules about this; it's a matter of what fits your situation. You may, for example, know a lot about investing, but work sixty-hour weeks. You just want to turn the whole thing over to somebody else, even if it means paying a high fee. In that case, you would favor the "in-person" route or, to save money, a comprehensive form of "over the phone." Let's take a look at the three options in the order stated:

1. IN PERSON

With a relatively large amount to invest (say, $250,000 or more), this option takes the form of face-to-face meetings. You delegate each of the five Giant Steps to someone who will be your on-going counselor. He or she is the one you call with questions and comments.

People who do this kind of counseling include professional planners and registered representatives of brokerage operations (in brokerage firms, insurance companies, banks, American Express). A key difference between the two is degree of specialization. Professional planners do nothing but counsel people for a fee, although some may also charge a commission. A registered representative carries out stock and bond trades in addition to counseling and usually works on commission. Some registered representatives are also professional planners.

Kinds of professional planners

Be careful. Planners come with various titles, and many states allow people of meager qualifications to call themselves financial planners. Here are four titles you can generally trust:

- *Certified Financial Planner* (CFP): trained in a broad range of financial and investment subjects. For a list of CFPs near you, call the International Board of Standards and Practices for Certified Financial Planners in Denver, Colorado: 800-282-7526.
- *Chartered Financial Consultant* (ChFC): usually has a background in life insurance and estate planning. Call the American College in Bryn Mawr, Pennsylvania: 610-526-1000.
- *Chartered Financial Analyst* (CFA): trained in security analysis and money management. Call the Association for Investment Management and Research in Charlottesville, Virginia: 804-977-6600.
- *Personal Financial Specialist* (PFS): may also be a certified public accountant and have a background in tax accounting. Call the American Institute of Certified Public Accountants in New York, New York: 212-596-6200.

Planners who earn the titles listed above undergo professional training and testing. Here's an excerpt, for example, from a catalog published by the College for Financial Planning:

The right to use the marks CFP® and Certified Financial Planner® is granted by the Certified Financial Planner Board of Standards, Inc., to those persons who have met its rigorous education standards, passed the CFP Board's CFP Certification Examination, satisfied a work experience requirement, and agreed to abide by the CFP Board Code of Ethics and Professional Responsibility.

In addition, those authorized to use this title must participate in a program of continuing education and supervised study.

Some CFPs and ChFCs are members of the National Association of Personal Financial Advisors ("NAPFA"). These planners are committed to the practice of charging only a fee. Commissions or any other payments that would tend to bias the planner are barred. In the words of the NAPFA media kit:

> In order to belong to NAPFA, a financial planner may not receive any economic benefit when a client implements that planner's recommendations, including (but not limited to) commissions, rebates, awards, finders' fees, and bonuses. NAPFA members also must avoid any circumstances which can create a possible conflict of interest.

Besides CFPs and ChFCs, NAPFA members include certified public accountants, attorneys, and people holding a master's degree in finance. Many planners hold two or more titles. They may have their own business or work for brokerage operations.

The compensation question

What counts most is the quality of the planner, not how he or she is paid. Still, it's worth remembering that a fee-based planner can recommend index funds and a buy-and-hold strategy without limiting his or her income. A commission-based planner has more to think about—and may be inclined to recommend non-index funds.

The argument for commission-based payment can be persuasive: The planner is paid, at least in part, by the fund families and life insurance companies, instead of the client. Superficially, it sounds like something for nothing. But many commission-based planners pay themselves up to 4.75 percent of your assets for trading mutual funds and up to 90 percent of the first year's premium on life insurance. On the investment side, that means your funds would have to do nearly 5 percent better than their relevant indexes, even without considering the tax advantage of index funds. Based on the evidence we've reviewed, that doesn't seem likely. On the other hand, if you like a particular high-cost planner and need him or her to take you through the investment process, then you do. No sense in pretending otherwise.

Fortunately, there's a way to be certain about a planner's sources of compensation up front: Ask the planner for his or her "ADV," which is a document that must be filed with the Securities and Exchange Commission. Part 1 of the ADV shows the planner's record of disciplinary actions; part 2 spells out the planner's sources of compensation.

What about stockbrokers?

Registered representatives (commonly called "stockbrokers") tend to be expensive compared with buying no-load funds directly from a fund company. Beyond that, there's a change in role you should keep in mind: When you trade stocks and bonds through a full-service brokerage firm, you need a registered representative to expedite trades for you; his or her investment recommendations are usually covered by the cost of the trade. In contrast, if you use a registered representative primarily as a long-term investment counselor, you need to evaluate him or her on that basis. Does this person have the credentials and experience to advise you on how to handle your life savings? Is he or she as well qualified as (say) a Certified Financial Planner? In the interest of fairness, I'm going to quote at length from a letter to a mutual fund magazine:

> Your biggest assumption is that someone can read your magazine and make an informed investment. The reality is that I see people every day who have followed the advice of the financial media and bought funds they never should own. What you get when you buy a loaded fund (at least if it's from me) is a careful analysis of goals, risk tolerance, and investment horizon. Only after I've determined these things will I make a recommendation. I

choose funds by what they hold and the management style, rather than any other criteria. The payout to me is of little consequence.

I also think that I will see a lot of fee-based business coming my way when the market turns. Why pay 3% to a planner when your portfolio is down? I provide all the same services as a financial advisor, and I get paid only for trades.

Registered Representative
(proudly)

The first paragraph of the letter strikes me as more solid than the second. Do-it-yourself investors do make serious mistakes, and many of them might be better off with professional guidance, even after accounting for higher costs. But I think there's a difference between an informed investor and one who is not informed. After you read this book, I believe you will be equipped to make intelligent investment decisions for yourself, especially if you create or buy a financial plan and investment plan. You may not need somebody to hold your hand. And you definitely don't need access to a brokerage operation's buy-sell-hold recommendations on stocks and bonds.

I question the second paragraph of the letter. The letter-writer might do everything a licensed planner does; I don't know. Some registered representatives are probably more effective than some financial planners. Whatever your choice, remember the now-familiar reservation about how a representative or planner is paid: It's usually in your best interest to work with someone who is financially free to recommend no-load index funds and a buy-and-hold strategy.

2. OVER THE PHONE

Some sources will take your information by phone and send you a hard copy of a personal plan. You may or may not deal with the same person on an ongoing basis. It depends in part on how much you have to invest and on what kind of relationship you want to have.

You can work this way with a registered representative of a brokerage operation. He or she sends you a questionnaire. You fill it out and return it. Your data goes through a software program and returns in the form of a financial plan, free. You are not obliged to go any further with the representative. He or she hopes to be compensated by buying and selling securities or funds for you, usually by commission, but sometimes by fee. As mentioned earlier, this can be relatively expensive over time.

If you'd rather not work that way, and you have a sizable amount to invest, you can go to some mutual fund families. Vanguard, for example, offers high-end plans (financial and investment) for a one-time fee of $500 per plan. You get a person to work with on a short-term basis. Or you can have Vanguard manage your portfolio on an ongoing basis for a fee that starts at .5 percent and works downward as the amount invested goes up (800-567-5162). It all happens over the phone.

3. ON YOUR OWN

This option is mostly for All-of-It-Myself people, but some versions may work for Some-of-It-Myself people. Again, it's a matter of what you're comfortable with.

Work sheets in booklets

Depending on how you handle it, this can be an easy way to get a plan. Nearly all large mutual fund families and brokerage operations offer a free retirement planning booklet with a "work sheet." This is a form that takes you through a series of steps that leads to a set of financial goals (see sample form in next chapter). If arithmetic fogs your brain, there's an easier route: Give the work sheet and booklet to your accounting firm. Since they already have most of your financial data, it should be relatively easy for them to fill in the blanks and give you a completed plan.

Also, don't forget the human resources department where

you work. They may be able to offer some guidance or at least refer you to reliable sources of financial planning information.

Web sites

This is one of the best ways to work on your own because you can do it interactively—useful, for example, when you want to know the effect of different rates of return. Go-to titles include "retirement planning," "college planning," "asset allocation," and anything with the word *portfolio.* Fidelity has one of the more comprehensive sites (www.fidelity.com). Click on "personal investing." Nearly all fund companies and well-known brokers have a Web site. The usual address is www.(name of company).com.

Do-it-yourself software kits

These usually come with one or more diskettes and a booklet. They take a sophisticated approach and are designed for the computer literate. Don't expect to breeze through them. They're usually more comprehensive than the work sheets, allowing you to include things like life insurance and real estate in a total plan—interactively. Typically, they include some degree of investment planning. *Available from:* large mutual fund companies and some other kinds of financial firms. The kits are available free or at low cost—$20 to $30.

Names and numbers

For your convenience, here's a list of prominent brokers and mutual fund companies. These companies tend to be heavy advertisers, offering various kinds of help, usually at no cost. The lists are not comprehensive, and no endorsement is implied. (Be aware that phone numbers change and financial services firms can merge.)

BROKERAGE OPERATIONS
American Express: 800-438-2384
Charles Schwab: 800-435-4000

Citicorp Investment Services: 800-721-1899
Merrill Lynch: 609-282-2424
Morgan Stanley Dean Witter: 212-703-4000
Prudential Life Insurance: 800-225-1852
Salomon Smith Barney: 800-327-6748

MUTUAL FUND COMPANIES
American Century: 800-345-2021
Dreyfus: 800-645-6561
Fidelity: 800-544-8888
Janus: 800-345-2021
Scudder: 800-225-2470
T. Rowe Price: 800-638-5660
Vanguard: 800-525-8983

GIANT STEP 2:
GET A PERSONAL INVESTMENT PLAN

Financial planning tells you *what you need;* investment planning tells you *how to get it.* A typical investment plan integrates the various factors that determine the way a particular individual should invest. It's designed to answer questions like these:

- How should I allocate my assets among the three major asset classes?
- Which subasset classes should I hold within each of the three major asset classes and in what proportion?
- Which fund family or families should I select?
- What criteria should drive my choice of funds?
- How should I change my portfolio as my needs change?

Investment plans have certain similarities to financial plans. They can be simple or complex, costly or free. And they're generally available from the same sources as financial plans:

- Financial planners
- Registered representatives in brokerage operations
- Financial planners in some mutual fund companies (by phone and mail)
- Do-it-yourself Web sites and software kits offered by mutual fund companies and brokerage operations
- Do-it-yourself work sheets in booklets offered by some mutual fund companies, brokerage operations, and fund supermarkets

The more work you're prepared to do yourself, the less you need to rely on others, such as financial planners.

Investment planning leads to a "balanced" portfolio. This means that money is allocated to a variety of asset classes in a way that addresses a particular investor's needs and goals. It's usually a good idea to get your investment plan from the same source as your financial plan, just for simplicity. The amount of guidance you receive tends to vary with how much you pay. Assume you have a simple plan. It may call for an allocation of 75 percent stocks and 25 percent bonds. (The assumption is that you use short-term bonds as cash.) You'll also be given the seventy-two year average return of that allocation, as well as its volatility (risk). Then you simply do the obvious:

- Compare the projected rate of return in the investment plan with the return specified in your financial plan.
- Decide if you can live with the stated degree of volatility.

If the investment plan return is too low or the volatility too high, you'll have to invest more or wait longer.

In a comprehensive investment plan, you'll get more guidance. Things like recommended subasset allocations, risk measured in a variety of ways, and detailed comparisons between the recommended allocations and those of any investments you may already have. Your plan may also include recommendations on what kinds of funds to buy, how much to invest in each, and a schedule for making the actual investments.

Malkiel's portfolios

In the last chapter, Burton Malkiel spells out his asset class allocations for three age groups. His recommendations include the name of one or more funds for each asset class, phone number, and expense ratio. Even if you're a none-of-it-myself person, reading these recommendations will give you insight and perhaps even persuade you to do some or all of the work yourself. If you're a Some-of-It-Myself or All-of-It-Myself person, you're well on your way to establishing a solid program as soon as you finish this book.

Yes you can

The fact is, successful investing can be a lot simpler than many sources make it out to be. It doesn't require an MBA and arcane analysis of individual securities, funds, or markets. Remember that up to 90 percent of your long-term result may come from how you allocate your money among the major asset classes—stocks, bonds, and cash (chapter 8). And within those classes, you're likely to do better by focusing on subasset classes (index funds) than on individual securities or individual non-index mutual funds. *As stated earlier, successful long-term investing is built on the idea of holding a diversified portfolio consisting mainly or entirely of index funds allocated to fit your situation.* You can look up the allocations for your age in this book or in many other sources. It's not quantum physics; you can do it.

SUMMARY

- To some extent, stock and bond markets are driven by rational concerns, but greed and fear often dominate, especially when the markets make a major move.

- In a process called "rotation," asset classes change their position in the ladder of investor preference. This is one reason a portfolio should contain a variety of asset classes.
- In a process called "regression-to-mean," the risk and return of any asset class tend to revert to historical norms.
- There are five major steps in the investment process: (1) get a financial plan; (2) get an investment plan; (3) build a balanced portfolio; (4) make the most of the tax laws; and (5) invest every month, starting as soon as possible, without trying to time the markets.
- To quantify needs, goals, and means, investors need structured planning. There are three types of plans: financial, investment, and estate. All three are sometimes referred to as "financial planning."
- Investors have a wide choice of sources for financial and investment planning, ranging from simple forms in company booklets to complex documents available from fund companies, financial planners, and brokerage operations.
- Informed and interested investors can build their own portfolios, and avoid the usual fees and commissions, by studying sample portfolios and applying the principles stated in this book.

COMING UP

The next chapter will be a continuation of this one. We will apply financial and investment planning to *investing for retirement*, perhaps today's most crucial issue in personal finance.

CHAPTER 10

Investing for Retirement

YOU MAY BE YOUNG AND SAVING FOR THE DOWN PAYMENT ON A home. You may be older and trying to accumulate money for your children's education. Or you may be older still and preparing for a second career. But *everybody* will have to look retirement in the eye and say, "Yes, I have enough money to deal with you."

Or not.

So in this chapter, we're going to apply what we've learned to that looming confrontation. If you have more immediate goals, hang in there. Many of the ideas used to prepare for retirement will also work for you. To begin with, it's vital to understand that *time can be more important than money,* as this example shows (adapted from Scudder's booklet, *Investing for Retirement*).

THE DIFFERENCE THAT TIME MAKES

Rate of return	8%
Rate of investment	$200 per month
Sum after 10 years	$36,840
Sum after 20 years	$118,580

Your gain after ten years is $12,840 ($36,840 minus the $24,000 you invested); after twenty years it's $70,580 ($118,580 minus $48,000). *By doubling the length of time, you more than quintupled your gain.* This is the power of compounding, building on a larger and larger base. No matter what stage of life you're in, now is the time to start or enlarge a disciplined investment program. The hard fact is, there are several reasons why your retirement may cost a lot more than you might imagine:

- *Long life.* You're probably going to live longer than your parents or grandparents. It used to be that people, especially men, died soon after they retired, or even before. Now a high percentage of people are living into their eighties, often in good health. So not only will you probably live a long time, you're also likely to be active—going places and doing things. Which costs money. Instead of just a few years of retirement, you may have to support two or three decades.
- *Inflation.* You're probably tired of hearing about this issue, but because of longer retirements—and the effects of compounding—it carries a big stick. According to Chicago-based Ibbotson Associates, an investment research company, inflation has averaged about 3 percent since 1926. But there have been long periods when the average rate was much higher. For the thirty-year period from 1965 through 1995, for example, the average was 6 percent. A little arithmetic shows how badly inflation can hurt: Assume a rate of 3 percent and remember what compounding means. You aren't subtracting 3 percent of your original retirement income every year; you're

subtracting 3 percent of a *constantly decreasing* amount. So if you started out with a comfortable amount every year, you could wind up twenty years later with not nearly enough to live on. (Don't despair. There's good news coming up.)

- *Early retirement.* You may decide you want to retire early to launch a second career or pursue an interest that means a lot to you. Or a future down-sizing may force you into early retirement. Whatever the cause, early retirement may lengthen your retirement years—and give inflation more time to eat away at your savings.

- *The decline in pensions.* American business has come to prefer defined contribution plans over pension plans. One reason is the cost—and its consequences. Underfunding at federally insured pensions early in 1997 was more than $50 billion. Which means there's a lot of employers who don't have enough money set aside to fund their pension plan. And replacement income from federal insurance stops at $31,000 a year. Your current job (or your next job) is more likely to offer a 401(k) or 403(b) than a pension plan. That puts the investment ball in your court. It's up to you to put enough money aside, choose good investment options, manage your progress, and handle your rollover properly when you change jobs. *All of which calls for a level of knowledge, discipline, and wealth your parents or grandparents didn't need.*

- *Less social security.* You've read all about it. No one knows how our lawmakers will resolve this issue, but the news is sobering. Changes already made: The minimum age to qualify for full benefits will increase steadily in the years ahead. Also, the taxable part of your social security payments has risen from 50 percent to 85 percent, if your total income (including half your social security income) is over $44,000 for married couples and $34,000 for singles. By the time today's babies reach sixty-five, they'll make up one-fifth of the population—unprecedented in the history of the world. So the help you get from social security is likely to go down.

- *Back-end tax.* One of these days, you'll start withdrawing money from your defined contribution plan and regular IRA accounts. The money you take out may be substantial enough to keep you in a high tax bracket—and subject to ordinary income tax rates, not the lower capital gains rate. This can be a serious hit. Check with your accountant or tax attorney.

On top of all that, you may have to invest for other goals, such as buying a home or paying college expenses. This pumps up the amount you need to save and may call for using different asset classes from those used for retirement (more on this to come). I don't mean to bring you down with a bunch of negative thoughts. It's just that there are realities we all have to confront, one way or another. Fortunately, there's an upside.

IS THERE ANY GOOD NEWS?

Yes. The compounding effect that makes inflation your enemy works in your favor when it comes to accumulating wealth. In fact, it works even harder, because your long-term investment return is likely to be a lot higher than the rate of inflation. So you're compounding at a higher rate. The table below shows four examples from Schwab's booklet, *Your Personal Guide to Retirement Planning:*

APPROXIMATE GROWTH OF $10,000
FOR 20 YEARS

6%	=	$32,000
8%	=	47,000
10%	=	67,000
12%	=	96,000

The percent figures refer to annualized rates of return. Each 2-percentage-point gain translates to a disproportionately larger result after twenty years. Example: Twelve percent is only two times larger than 6 percent, but the result after twenty years is three times larger. This is another example of the power of compounding, your best friend in the struggle to prepare for retirement or other long-term objectives.

IS INFLATION
ON THE ROPES?

There may be more good news. Some economists think we may be in for a long period of low inflation. In his paper *Economics and Portfolio Strategy* (March 1997), economist Peter L. Bernstein (Peter L. Bernstein, Inc., New York) points out that "the disappearance of inflationary pressures has become a worldwide rather than just a domestic phenomenon." The essence of his argument is that built-in, long-term inflation is not a natural state of an economy. He draws a clear contrast between inflationary pressures before 1980 and after 1980. Among the more recent factors holding down inflation:

Worldwide disinflation
Intensification of global competition
Rapid pace of technological change
Basic changes in central bank structures

Bernstein is not alone in forecasting lower inflation. But not everyone agrees with his optimistic point of view, and, in any case, the long-term investor can't afford to rely on the possibility of long-term low inflation. What if the forecast is wrong? A series of regional wars, for example, could give inflation a boost. Many sources of financial planning use 4 percent for planning, and some use even higher figures. So whether you take an optimistic or conservative view of inflation, preparing for retirement is still a high priority challenge. How do we meet it?

WHAT IT'S LIKE

I'm going to get surreal to convey the real world of investing for retirement. Imagine you're standing near the bank of a rain-swollen river that's about to flood the surrounding countryside. At the same time, you know that on the high ground across the river, there's a great party going on. You can even hear the thump of a thousand-watt amplifier pounding out bass notes through giant speakers. Not only that, but there's free booze, great food, and prizes just for showing up.

You really want to get to that high ground. But the only way is to wade across a fast-flowing stream with muddy water. You can't see the bottom, and you know the depth varies. There are wide, shallow spots that look safe, except that the land is flat there, and the river is fast invading those areas. In other places, the stream is narrow, and it looks as though you might cross quickly. But those places could be too deep, maybe dangerous.

In the end, you choose a place of average depth and width. You plan your route carefully, find a sturdy stick of the right height to help you wade, and step into the stream. Most of the way, you make steady progress. But the bottom is uneven. Every so often you hit a few deep spots and think, for just an instant, of turning back. But you have confidence in your route, and you know your staff will hold up. You stay the course and arrive safely at the opposite shore, where you easily get to the good times.

By now, you should be able to recognize familiar points in this (somewhat attenuated) metaphor:

- Inflation is relentless.
- A low return may not keep you ahead of inflation.
- Going for the highest returns could be dangerous.
- It pays to go for the average (index) return.
- The markets are unpredictable.

- You need a plan.
- You need a portfolio (the wading stick).
- The markets fluctuate.
- It pays to stick to your plan.

With all that in mind, let's see what's involved in working up a financial and investment plan for retirement, which I'll refer to as a "retirement plan." We'll start with retirement planning booklets, because the better ones make a useful complement to this book.

Oddly, some of the biggest names on Wall Street have some of the worst booklets. They've spared no expense in using fancy formats with gold and silver inks. But the booklets are designed to impress rather than inform. They're so decorative, the reader doesn't know where to look first, and the text is hard to follow. Among the dozens of choices, I think there are at least three that stand out. I suggest you get at least one of them, even if you're going to buy your financial and investment plans from another source. Here's a short review of each:

THREE GOOD SOURCES OF RETIREMENT INFORMATION

Scudder's Investing for Retirement

Easily the most accessible guide I've seen. Designed to *invite* reading, not just make it possible. Great care is taken to make things as simple and clear as possible (without being simplistic). The writing is arguably the best among the booklets I reviewed; you can sit down and read it without feeling as though you're at the dentist. It's a good choice for anyone, especially beginning investors or those who find investment talk off-putting. Included are a few pages that show you how to work up a limited, but useful, personal financial plan. (Scudder, Stevens & Clark, sixty-four pages, free, 800-225-2470.)

Schwab's *Your Personal Guide to Retirement Planning*

Possibly the best short guide (thirty pages). It doesn't try for style or elegance; the design and writing are deliberately functional. The text sticks to essential information—no frills, nothing to get in the way. It assumes the reader has at least a basic understanding of investment issues and does little in the way of hand-holding. On this point, it probably matches the profile of the average Schwab customer (which I assume to be Do Some of It Myself or Do All of It myself). It's a good choice for those who fit those profiles and want a quick but solid review of the retirement planning process. Includes easy-to-follow forms for financial and investment planning. (Charles Schwab, free, 800-435-4000.)

The Vanguard Retirement Investment Guide

Designed to be the gold standard of retirement planning guides. It provides thorough, useful guidance on nearly all the investment topics related to retirement planning, including how to save, how to invest, social security, selling a home, and tax strategies. The section on financial planning is the best I've seen. In thirteen pages, it takes you through the entire planning process. It provides another five pages of numerical factors that make it easy to personalize a complete plan to your exact circumstances. Written for people who want an in-depth understanding of retirement planning issues. (Vanguard, 226 pages, $10, 800-662-7447.)

Of course, these and many other sources also offer interactive financial planning on Web sites.

With all this in mind, here's a quick review of the retirement planning process:

THE MONEY YOU'LL NEED

Find out how much you're spending per year. Add your credit card charges and the total of all the checks you write. Then add a generous amount for your cash expenses (they're probably bigger than you think). You may find this a bit tedious, but it's an essential part of arriving at a target amount for retirement or any other objective. This process also highlights places where you can trim your spending and liberate more money to invest.

Account for inflation. As mentioned, the old standard of 4 percent may be too high. Still, when you apply a lower rate over a realistic number of years, you come up with a sobering fact:

> Assume an average inflation rate of 3 percent for forty years (twenty years before retirement and twenty years after). Even with this optimistic rate, an income of $60,000 a year drops to $18,393 a year in real purchasing power.

Could you live on that little? If not, where would you get help? How would you manage? Inflation, even at a moderate rate, can kick you in the shins. We're told that the Consumer Price Index (CPI) overstates the amount of inflation. Maybe. But people tend to need more medical treatment as they get older, and health care costs continue to grow faster than the index as a whole—something to keep in mind, even if you think you'll always have health insurance.

Take 70 percent of the inflated amount. Roughly speaking, this figure gives you a retirement goal in dollars for the day you retire. (Of course, inflation continues *after* you retire.) The 70 percent number isn't carved in stone; it's just a generally accepted rule of thumb for what most people spend in retirement, compared with what they spent before. Whatever the figure, it's reasonable to assume you'll spend less in retirement than you're spending now. Things that will probably cost you less include:

- *Income and sales taxes.* You may be in a lower tax bracket and spending less on taxable goods and services.
- *Mortgage payments.* If you're lucky, you'll have paid off your mortgage. Or you'll be ready to live in a smaller, lower-cost home.
- *Education.* The kids, if any, should be out of college. (Notice I said "should.")
- *Life insurance.* You'll have reached the point where cash values are high enough to pay the premiums (depending on the type of policy). Or you may not need life insurance.
- *Dressing for work, commuting to work.* You've probably got all the business clothes you need. And forget the cost of snaking your way through traffic jams to get to The Place That Pays You.

Those savings may be nice to think about, but they don't change the basic picture. If you have, say, twenty years before you retire and another twenty years after that, you're looking at *forty years* of inflation. So don't be surprised if your retirement goal turns out to be an intimidating number. Fortunately, there are other numbers.

THE MONEY YOU'LL EARN

As we go through these points, you'll notice they call for predicting things that are hard to predict. Don't let that stop you. The estimates don't have to be exact, and you'll get a lot of help from your planning source (work sheets, software, Web site, or person).

Add any defined benefit income you expect to earn. To refresh your memory, a defined benefit pension plan provides a definite amount of monthly income, paid by your employer and based on your income, length of employment, and other factors. It's a good idea to make sure you understand all the terms and conditions. What happens if you leave the company? How many years does it take before all the money in your account is yours? Unfortunately, there's no way to tell whether you'll be employed when that magic date arrives. You've probably heard those horror stories about people missing the deadline by a few weeks or months and winding up with no lasting income to show for many years of work.

Add the amount you expect to get from any defined contribution plan you may have. Types of plans include 401(k), 403(b) (for employees of nonprofit companies), 457 (for government workers), individual IRA, SEP-IRA (for small businesses), and Keogh (for self-employed people).

Add the amount of any inheritance you expect to receive. This is tough to figure, but a rough estimate will do. The point is not to leave out a potentially substantial sum from your plan.

Add the social security payments you expect to receive. You can get this number by calling Social Security at 800-537-7005 or by scanning the tables in the booklets we reviewed.

Add expected income from any other source. Examples include investments you've made on your own, real estate, inheritances, proceeds from the sale of a business, and any work you may do after retiring. You or your planning source will have to figure out what all that will be worth, allowing for inflation, interest income, and growth.

A HYPOTHETICAL PLAN

We've covered the basic components. Now let's look at how an actual plan would be developed. The one that follows is taken from Vanguard's booklet. But just to make things interesting, let's assume it's your plan—that all the numbers represent your personal situation.

Items 1 through 6 are straightforward. But notice the investment return in Item 7—just 8 percent. Why not 15 percent or 20 percent, like the numbers you've seen in the mid-nineties? Be-

WORKSHEET: HOW MUCH SHOULD I SAVE FOR RETIRMENT?

	Example	Your Own Situation
Your Retirement Income Goal and Benefits		
1. Your current income	$80,000	_____
2. Your retirement income goal (70% to 80% of line 1)	$56,000	_____
3. Social Sercurity benefits	$24,000	_____
4. Pension	$10,000	_____
5. Annual shortfall (Line 2 − Line 3 − Line 4)	$22,000	_____
6. Current retirement savings	$34,000	_____
Your Assumptions		
7. Investment return	8%	_____
8. Years until retirement	20	_____
9. Retirement period (in years)	25	_____
Retirement Factors		
10. Inflation factor (Table A)	2.19	_____
11. Capital needed for retirement (Table B)	16.49	_____
12. Inflation adjustment for pension (Table C)	4.96	_____
13. Investment growth (Table D)	4.66	_____
14. Current retirement savings factor (Table E)	.0150	_____
Your Income Needs		
15. Annual income goal at retirement (Line 2 × Line 10)	$123,000	_____
16. Annual income shortfall at retirement (Line 5 × Line 10)	$48,000	_____
17. Additional capital needed at retirement (Line 16 × Line 11)	$792,000	_____
Inflation Adjustment		
18. Value of pension at retirement (Line 4 × Line 10)	$22,000	_____
19. Inflation adjustment for pension (Line 18 × Line 12)	$109,000	_____
Value of Current Savings at Retirement		
20. Current savings at retirement (Line 6 × Line 13)	$158,000	_____
Your Retirement Savings Goal		
21. Net savings needed (Line 17 + Line 19 − Line 20)	$743,000	_____
22. Current annual savings needed (Line 21 × Line 14)	$11,000	_____
23. Percent of current annual income (Line 22 ÷ Line 1)	14%	_____

Note: Figures in example are rounded and assume a 4% annual rate of inflation.

cause this is a real-world example. It assumes you have a balanced and diversified portfolio, which trades the hope of terrific gains in return for long-term reliability, allowing for regression to mean.

Items 10 through 14 are multipliers obtained from tables in the back of the Vanguard booklet. Items 16 and 17 reveal the income shortfall and the additional capital needed at retirement—numbers that may make you swallow hard. Items 18 and 19 show the effect of inflation, while Item 20 brings a bright spot in terms of how much your current savings are expected to grow.

The most vital information comes in items 21 through 23. You see the lump sum you'll have to accumulate and finally, what is probably the most useful number, the amount you have to save every year, expressed in dollars and as a percent of your pretax income.

When you compare the money you'll need with the money you'll earn, you may find a gap (or maybe a canyon). Most people do. If you have a family, you may find it hard just to break even, without trying to save 14 percent of your gross income. (The average American saves only 5 percent, according to the August 18, 1997, issue of *Fortune*.) And don't forget, 14 percent of your gross will be a significantly larger part of your *after-tax* income. You are face to face with the "Money Gap."

As an alternative to completing a form like this, you might prefer to use a computer application. A good one is the "Retirement Planning Analyzer" from T. Rowe Price ($19.95, 800-541-7861). As we've seen, most of the large mutual fund families and brokerage operations have similar products.

HOW TO CLOSE THE MONEY GAP

Common sense says you have at least six ways to close the Money Gap:

1. *Earn more while you're working.*

   Being an employee used to mean that you worked for a *specific company*. That idea is limping on its last legs. Now you think in terms of working for an entire *industry*. The industry is your employer. Thinking this way helps you focus on what you need to do to stay mobile—and well paid.

2. *Retire later.*

   There's no law that says you have to quit working for money at any particular age. You may be able to continue your career, or with persistent hunting, get part-time work you enjoy. *Caution:* Some of the money you earn between the ages of sixty-two and seventy will be deducted from your social security benefits. For details, call Social Security at 800-772-1213.

3. *Plan to spend less during retirement.*

   Instead of going to the south of France for a few weeks, go to the south of Florida or points west. This doesn't have to be a terrible thing. Often, it's just a matter of adjusting your perception of what it takes to make you happy.

4. *Get a reverse mortgage.*

   If you own your home, you can arrange to convert some of your equity (the unmortgaged portion) to a monthly income. It works like a mortgage loan, only in reverse. You borrow against the value of your home, but instead of gradually *paying off* the loan, you gradually *receive* the amount of the loan. A reverse mortgage has some disadvantages, especially to your heirs. For more information, and a list of vendors who provide reverse mortgages, call the American Association of Retired Persons, 202-434-2277.

5. *Spend less to invest more.*

   As you look ahead to retirement, there are lots of uncertainties. But there's one thing you know for sure: *If you spend less, you can invest more.* That decision is within your current control. It may help to remember that when you spend a discretionary dollar before retirement, you're not just spending the dollar; *you're spending what that dollar could earn before you re-*

tire. Depending on your age, that could mean shrinking your nest egg by $5 for every $1 you spend.

Which may mean you need to spend more efficiently. *Money* offers a book called *Dollar Pinching: A Consumer's Guide to Smart Spending,* by Shelly Branch (800-633-9970). Also, you might want to call Money 2000 (no connection with *Money* magazine). Offered by several state universities, it's a practical program that educates people in how to save money (202-720-5119).

And then there's credit card debt. Think of it as a mind-altering drug. With an interest rate of 20 percent or more, it drives you to spend hundreds of dollars a year to feed a bad habit. Think also of what a mutual fund would have to earn to return 20 percent a year, *after taxes.* The answer may strengthen your motivation.

6. **Minimize the pain.**

By universal agreement, one of the most useful gap-closing techniques is to make saving automatic. Giving up what you never had is a lot easier than paying it out. The basic idea is to set aside the same amount every month. It's simple if your employer has a 401(k) or similar plan. But that may not be enough. Outside an employer's plan, you can authorize your bank to make regular deductions from your checking or money market account and wire the money to your investment supplier.

SUMMARY

- Accumulating enough money for retirement is probably the biggest financial challenge you will face (especially if you've depleted your assets by paying for your children's education).
- There are several reasons why retirement may cost a lot more than it used to (even though inflation may stay at a moderate level).

- Schwab, Scudder, and Vanguard offer good booklets on retirement. Software kits and mutual fund Web sites are also helpful. Or you may prefer to hire a professional planner.
- Studying a hypothetical financial plan will help you do your own plan—or evaluate a plan done for you.
- You're likely to have a Money Gap between what you need at retirement and what your current situation is likely to provide.
- There are at least six ways to close the Money Gap; an automatic investment program is probably the best.

CHAPTER 11

Giant Step 3:
Build Your Portfolio

THERE ARE FEW THINGS MORE SATISFYING THAN REALIZING you've made $50,000—and didn't lift a finger to get it. All you did was make a few good investment decisions, the most important of which was how to structure your portfolio. Let's see what that's all about.

GIANT STEP 3:
INVEST WITH A PORTFOLIO

This book often uses the terms "diversified" and "balanced." To refresh your memory, "diversified" refers to a broad mix of *asset classes* (not just a broad mix of securities). "Balanced" means allocating the asset classes to reflect your situation. It's vital to understand this point:

> Don't invest with *individual* stocks, bonds, or mutual funds. Invest with a diversified portfolio of index funds, balanced to fit your needs and goals.

This is a Big Idea, often overlooked with all the focus on hot stocks and the past performance of mutual funds. As we saw earlier, the division of your assets among the major asset classes is likely to determine more of your performance than any other single factor.

Many people invest *without* creating an appropriate portfolio. Those with a tax-advantaged plan at work tend to buy a couple of funds that seem safe. Those with taxable accounts typically buy a few funds that did well last year and maybe some stocks that are supposed to double in six months. The worst thing that can happen to these people (financially speaking) is to get lucky. It makes them think they know what they're doing.

The focus on portfolios is crucial because of your needs as a long-term investor. You're not going to play the markets, trying to buy at the bottom and sell at the top. What then? Common sense says to do whatever will put the odds in your favor. That starts with index funds and continues with ideas like diversification, asset class rotation, and the human inability to predict the future. All this points to a specific attitude:

> I don't want to go for the *highest* return, because that will mean the highest risk. I need the *most reliable* return, consistent with enough growth to meet the goals of my financial plan.

This is the voice of reality. A voice that recognizes the difference between a bet and an investment. It may be tempting to go for the highest possible returns. But as we've seen, that strategy is almost always accompanied by the highest volatility. If you're in a position to live with that, fine. Most of us are not. At the same time, you need to accept enough risk to have a reasonable chance of achieving the goals stated in your financial plan.

The investment principles in this chapter apply whether you invest on your own, through your employer's plan, or both. You need to look at all your accounts as a single portfolio to make sure your total asset allocation is where you want it.

BACKGROUND FOR PORTFOLIO BUILDING

There are certain things you should know before we get into serious portfolio-building. Let's have a look at three of them: risk, the history of the markets, and diversification.

1. "How much risk should I take?"

Since the markets tend to reward risk, the level of risk you choose tends to determine your long-term return. But when the markets go south, risk can test your nerves to the limit—literally keep you awake at night. Which is enough to make it a key issue. But there's another point: *There is no escape from risk.* You can't dodge it by keeping all your money in CDs or money market accounts; inflation may consume nearly all your gains. You can't duck it by putting all your money in bonds. The long-term return after inflation may be too low to reach your investment goal. Which brings us to stocks, which have been rewarding, but notoriously volatile. What to do? The answer is to adjust your portfolio's risk level to fit your personal situation. We'll look at five ways to do that:

- Risk tolerance
- Age

- Time horizon
- Portfolio size
- Financial plan

RISK TOLERANCE

Every financial plan questionnaire I've ever seen has a section where the provider tries to evaluate the investor's risk tolerance. The investor may be asked about his or her general risk tolerance, as well as investment-related risk tolerance. Once labeled (I picture a letter stamped on the investor's forehead), the investor is usually shown an array of portfolios, each of which is characterized with names like "Aggressive," "Moderate," or "Conservative," sometimes with variations on each.

I have doubts about "risk tolerance" as a valid way to select a level of volatility. To start with, I don't believe a dozen or so questions prepared by a financial company can reliably measure a person's ability to handle stress. Human beings are not that simple. If I choose "conservative," does it mean I'm a wimp? If I go for "aggressive," does it mean I'm reckless? Are my general attitudes toward risk a reliable guide to my reaction to financial risk? If I think I know what to choose today, will I think the same tomorrow? It's all too subjective.

Can you imagine going to a person who barely knows the difference between a stock and a bond and saying, "Okay, Joe, do you want your investment portfolio to be Aggressive, Moderate, or Conservative? Or would you prefer Moderately Aggressive?"

"Huh?" The vast majority of people simply don't know what posture they should take; they haven't a clue. But here's what is known: The fear of losing money is far stronger than the desire to make money. (Markowitz used this point in developing Modern Portfolio Theory.) The result is that millions of people with tax-deferred plans choose a risk-reward level that is too low to meet their needs. This fact has captured the attention of employers, who are working hard to get their employees into more aggressive investments—not necessarily because of empathetic concerns. Many are afraid of class-action suits as employees reach retirement age and find their retirement plan doesn't give them enough to live on.

Exception: If you're *very* uncomfortable with the level of risk implied by your portfolio's rate of return, move down a notch. It's important to feel comfortable with your portfolio.

AGE

This works fairly well. It does so because it's objective and, usually, a good measure of a person's financial situation. Young people often have lighter financial burdens than older people. Beyond that, age works because of simple arithmetic. Young people have decades to ride out down markets and wait for the next up market. Also, they have earnings from employment to cushion the blow of a bear market. Retired people may have neither. You can't rely on a quick recovery like the one after the 1987 crash (six months). It took many *years* before large stocks recovered from the bear market of 1973. People at or near retirement age can't accept that kind of long-term down market. Overall, age is a good measure of your ability to assume risk, but it has one limitation: It can't tell you if a particular risk-reward level is likely to meet your quantified retirement goals.

TIME FRAME

The shorter your time horizon, the more conservative your portfolio needs to be. If you're investing to get the down payment for a home or business, you probably have a date in mind; your portfolio has to be on the money at that time. Intermediate-term corporate bond funds may be as aggressive you want to get. If you're investing for your children's education, you may have more time—ten or twelve years, let's say. In that time frame, your portfolio can include stock funds. Beyond ten years, you can afford to be even more aggressive. How *much* more depends largely on your age and other factors. If you're under thirty, you may want an *all*-stock portfolio; if you're forty or more, it may be prudent to include bond funds.

PORTFOLIO SIZE

The amount of risk you take depends, to a certain extent, on the amount of money you have. Someone with $200,000 has to be more conservative than someone with $2 million. The richer person has enough cushion to ride out market corrections.

FINANCIAL PLAN

With all due respect to the previous criteria, the best is probably the most obvious:

What is the lowest risk you can take that's consistent with reaching the goals stated in your financial plan?

This approach is simple and quantitative. To make it clear, let's go back to the financial plan in the previous chapter. There were four key assumptions:

1. 8% return
2. 20 years before retirement
3. 25 years in retirement
4. 4% inflation

As mentioned, 4 percent may be high, but let's go with it for consistency. With all that as a given, you need to invest $11,000 a year—14 percent of your gross annual income—to reach your goal of $743,000. On the other hand, suppose you get lucky, and your income increases more than you expect. You might want to contribute more per month and take *less* risk. Or suppose you decide you just can't save $11,000 a year, and you want to take *more* risk in hopes of earning a higher return. With these and other possibilities in mind, you ask your financial planning source to give you a range of options, *each* of which is estimated to reach $743,000:

- Invest a specific amount *more* than $11,000 a year at 7 percent.
- Invest $11,000 a year at 8 percent (as in sample plan).

- Invest a specific amount *less* than $11,000 a year at 9 percent or more.

In this context, you can afford to think about whether you want to be conservative, moderate, or aggressive—for a simple reason: *You now have the security of knowing that all your choices have the potential to achieve your goal.* That's a lot different, and better, than choosing a risk level in a vacuum. It makes your risk decision part of a total system objectively structured to meet a dollar-specific goal.

2. The seven-decade history of the securities markets

One of the key elements in building a portfolio is the history of how stocks, bonds, and cash (including short-term bonds) have performed since 1926. Allowing for periodic deviations, like the middle and late nineties, these figures may give you a rough idea of what you can expect in the long-term future. "Stnd. Dev." refers to standard deviation.

RETURNS, INFLATION, AND RISK 1926–1996

	COMPOUND ANNUAL RETURN	RISK (STND. DEV.)	RETURN PER UNIT OF STND. DEV.
Small-company stocks	12.7	33.9	.37
Large-company stocks	11.0	20.3	.54
Long-term corporate bonds	5.7	8.7	.65
Long-term government bonds	5.2	9.2	.56
Intermediate-term government bonds	5.3	5.7	.93
Treasury bills	3.8	3.2	N/A
Inflation	3.1	4.5	N/A

These figures are adapted from © *Stocks, Bonds, Bills, and Inflation 1997 Yearbook*™, Ibbotson Associates, Chicago.

Caution: These are *average* rates of return, concealing many wide swings. That long period of time is reassuring, but by no means a guarantee. Future returns could be worse or better. On the other hand, the numbers in this table are not mere shots in the dark. Most industry professionals use these numbers for financial and investment planning.

This table tells us a lot about the relative performance of various asset classes over seven decades. For example:

- Small-company stocks have outperformed large-company stocks by 18 percent.
- Large-company stocks have outperformed long-term government bonds by 91 percent.
- After inflation, T-bills returned .6 percent; long-term government bonds returned only 2 percent, which explains why most people need stocks to build a portfolio.
- Return per unit of standard deviation reveals differences among the relative performance of subasset classes. Examples: Large-company stocks give you more return per unit of risk than do small-company stocks. Intermediate-term bonds are a better deal, in terms of risk/reward, than long-term bonds. That doesn't mean you buy only large-cap funds and intermediate-term bond funds. But it could affect their relative weight in your portfolio.

Usually, you pay for higher returns with higher risk. Over the seventy-year period, there have been many times when these generalizations were not true. These include long periods when large stocks outperformed small stocks, as well as times when bonds outperformed both large and small stocks.

3. The need for diversity

We've discussed asset class rotation, regression to mean, the inability to predict the future, and the principles of Modern Portfolio Theory. All these ideas (and more) point us toward investing in a broad range of asset classes. Since we don't know what's going to happen, we need to be ready for anything. But that doesn't mean we have to be totally defensive. It's encouraging to remember that the stock market has gone up an average of three years out of four for the last seventy years. We also know that the amount of risk you can take for the long term is related to the goals of your financial plan.

With all this behind us, we can now discuss how to allocate major asset classes and how to buy funds to build your portfolio.

STOCKS, BONDS, CASH: HOW MUCH OF EACH?

As we've seen, the way your money is divided among the three major asset classes could determine more than 90 percent of your portfolio return. Fortunately, most industry professionals agree (roughly) on how the major asset classes should be allocated by age. To start, people are usually divided into three or four age groups, more or less like this: 30–44, 45–64, and 65 plus. The first age group is often referred to as "accumulation years;" the second, as "transition;" and the third, as "retired." These age groups represent the so-called "life cycle" that has become the basis for setting up mutual funds with instant portfolios.

The big question now is, "Based on these age groups, what split among stocks, bonds, and cash should I use?" Burton Malkiel answers the question, complete with fund recommendations for subasset classes. For now, we'll stick with his age-related allocations of stocks, bonds, and cash.

ASSET ALLOCATION
BY MAJOR ASSET CLASS

AGE	STOCK FUNDS	BOND FUNDS	CASH OR SHORT-TERM BONDS
30	80%	15%	5%
48	73	22	5
65+	60	30	10

Reading down the stock and bond fund columns, you can see how the percentage of stock funds gradually *decreases*, while the percentage of bond funds *increases*; the portfolio is changing from a *growth* orientation to an *income* orientation. It's also decreasing in *potential return*, while it increases in *reliability*. The change in emphasis from stock funds to bond funds reflects the change in priorities as people get older. As discussed, you can fine-tune these percentages with at least the following factors:

- *Your age.* Example: Look at age forty-eight. If you're significantly younger, you might want to be more aggressive than if you're older than forty-eight.
- *Time frame.* If you need to have a certain sum within a relatively short time—for college expenses, for example—it's prudent to be more conservative.
- *Size of cushion.* If you're well off financially, you can afford to be more aggressive—you can fall back on your cushion.
- *Family status.* If you're single, you can usually afford to take more risk than someone with a family.

A more aggressive approach

Just so you know, there are some advisors who point out there's no stone wall between "before sixty-five" and "after sixty-five." Life goes on, probably for a long time. That being the case, why not hold a relatively large portion of stock funds—say, 80 percent instead of 40 percent? Why not, the theory goes, enjoy the higher return that stock funds usually provide and draw on the gain in principal? The logical answer is that it depends on how much of a cushion you have—substantial savings, a pension, income from a part-time job, and so on. If you live well within your means, you can weather a bear market and still have enough to sustain your lifestyle. If you live close to the edge, you can't afford to wait, and you have to be more cautious.

SIX WAYS TO BUILD YOUR PORTFOLIO

You now have some idea about how to allocate major asset classes. With that background, let's review a variety of ways to buy an off-the-shelf portfolio or build your own. As we go through this, it may be helpful to keep in mind whether you're a None of It Myself, Some of It Myself, or All of It Myself (see chapter 9).

1. Hire a professional

If you have enough money—and that changes from source to source—you can simply hire someone to do everything for you. It could be, for example, a Certified Financial Planner or a registered representative from a brokerage operation. The cost depends on how much you have to invest, but generally ranges from 1 percent to 2 percent or more of assets *every year*. Over time, that can add up to a considerable amount. Also, if security prices fall, and stay down for several years, that 1 percent to 2 percent may seem totally pointless: "Why am I paying money to lose money?" On the other hand, if you really need someone to help you start and stay with an appropriate investment program—if that's the only way to get action—he or she can be worth all the money you pay. In any event, try to get someone who works on a fee-only basis, as discussed in the preceding chapter.

2. Buy a life cycle fund

This is a fund of funds, index or non-index, blended to reflect the needs of a specific age group. Ideally, you get broad diversification and a reasonably good fit to your situation. Life cycle funds are popular with investors; they simplify what could be a complex decision. But it pays to shop. Look for *index* life cycle funds that track substantially *all* the U.S. stock markets, *all* the U.S. bond markets, international stocks, and emerging markets. Why all? To deal with asset class rotation and regression to mean. You don't know which asset classes will be the future winners and losers, so buy a broad variety.

There are a few potential downsides to life cycle funds. Typically, they consist entirely of funds from a single mutual fund company, and the allocations for your age group may not fit your personal situation.

Available in no-load form from fund families, including: Dreyfus (800-782-6620), Fidelity (800-544-8888), Schwab (800-266-5623), T. Rowe Price (800-638-5660), and Vanguard (800-662-7447).

3. Buy an automatic life cycle fund

This type of fund takes the life cycle idea a step further. Wells Fargo, for example, has a set of non-index funds called "LifePath Funds" (800-222-8222), which automatically change the blend of stocks, bonds, and cash in certain years that you can specify in advance. That way, your portfolio keeps up with your age (though not necessarily with your individual financial needs). Fidelity (800-544-8888) has a similar product. Their "Freedom Funds" are managed to specific target years: 2000, 2010, 2020, and 2030, plus a fifth fund that's managed for income. All the funds consist of *non*-index Fidelity funds. With that in mind, be sure to check on the expense ratio before you buy.

4. Buy a balanced fund

Here you get a two-part mixture of domestic stocks and bonds. The typical split is 60 percent stocks, 40 percent bonds. The attraction: In a single fund, you get a blend that should perform fairly well in a wide variety of market conditions. The downside: If you're young, it's hard to find a balanced fund with a high enough proportion of stocks. And if you're retired, it's hard to find one with a high enough proportion of bonds. Also, most balanced funds don't include foreign securities.

Available from: All large mutual fund companies and brokerage operations. Try to find companies that offer *index* balanced funds, especially those that track broad indexes. (Of course, you can create your own balanced fund simply by combining a "total stock market" index fund and a "total bond market" index fund. It would have the virtues of simplicity and very low cost.)

5. Buy a blend of funds from one company

This type of product addresses the downside of two-part balanced funds. Some fund families (Fidelity, Scudder, T. Rowe Price, and Vanguard, for example) offer a blend of their own funds that amounts to a balanced portfolio. Fidelity's entry has fifteen funds; T. Rowe Price's, seven; Vanguard's, nine—all in one fund of funds. It's an instant portfolio. You get a broad spectrum of equity funds, from conservative to moderately aggressive, plus a range of fixed income funds. Unlike the funds of funds described in point 2, these are not necessarily keyed to particular age groups.

Also, they are *not* index funds. The managers decide, within narrow limits, how to vary the proportion of each major asset class. The stock portion generally goes from 60 percent to 70 percent of assets, bonds from 20 percent to 30 percent, and money market from 10 percent to 20 percent. A downside for some investors: You're restricted to the funds of one company; you can't shop for component funds from a variety of sources. Also, these funds are not specifically tailored to your age group. But if a fund fits your needs, it gives you single-source simplicity with broad diversification.

One other thing: Some funds-of-funds charge extra for assembling the subfunds—usually 1 percent to 1.5 percent on top of their regular operating expenses. The total can amount to 3.5 percent in annual charges, not counting any sales charges. Based on the evidence we're seen, it's hard to imagine how a fund with that level of burden could compete with a similar package of index funds.

Notice: T. Rowe Price, Scudder, and Vanguard *do not* have a surcharge; you get the blended funds at the same cost as unblended funds. Call T. Rowe Price at 800-638-5660. Scudder at 800-225-2470. Vanguard at 800-662-7447.

6. Buy a blend of broad-based index funds

This is a good route if you want to assemble a portfolio on your own. Buy at least four components to get adequate diversification:

1. *Domestic stocks:* Buy a fund that tracks a broad index such as the Wilshire 5,000 or the Russell 3,000, both of which represent essentially all the U.S. stock markets—large cap, small cap, growth and value, and so on.
2. *Foreign stocks:* Buy a fund that tracks the standard indexes for European, Asian, and emerging market stocks.
3. *Domestic bonds:* Buy a fund that tracks the Lehman Brothers Aggregate Bond Index, which represents all the U.S. bond markets, including treasuries, mortgage-backed, corporate, and government agencies. The blend has a maturity horizon

of eight or nine years—like intermediate-term bonds. (Municipal bond funds are not included, so if you want those, you'll have to buy them separately.)

4. *A money market or short-term bond fund.* A bank money market will serve the purpose, but most mutual fund families have a range of money market funds that pay a little more, although they are not federally insured. Be careful about expenses. They're a larger part of the return on a money market or short-term bond fund than on stock funds. There's no need to pay more than .35 percent.

A few companies offer all four of these types of funds under their own name. Two examples: Charles Schwab (800-435-4000) and Vanguard (800-562-1371). The Schwab line-up includes:

- *Schwab 1,000*, which tracks Schwab's own index of the 1,000 largest U.S. companies
- *Schwab Small-Cap Index Fund*, which tracks Schwab's index of the *next* 1,000 largest U.S. companies
- *Schwab International Index Fund*, which tracks the Schwab International Index, including 350 of the world's largest non-domestic companies
- *Schwab Total Bond Market Fund*, which tracks the Lehman Brothers Government-Corporate Aggregate Bond Index

Each of these funds is no-load and has a reasonable expense ratio (from .46 to .58). You can get a well-diversified portfolio of index funds with one phone call.

WHAT ABOUT NON-INDEX FUNDS?

You may have noticed: All along I've used the phrase "consisting mainly or entirely of index funds." Depending on your situation—and especially if you're an All-of-It-Myself person—you might want to add some non-index funds to your portfolio. The key is to understand which asset classes to choose. When you buy a non-index fund, you're buying management. Therefore, it seems to me, buy into asset classes where the markets are less efficient and where management might make a difference: small-cap or emerging markets, for example. If you can stand the volatility, and do your homework, you might find a few managers who have spotted an opportunity before their peers. To improve your chances, favor funds with a small number of stocks: twenty to forty. You want to be sure your managers have enough time to keep close watch on their fledglings. And don't forget about costs. Trading emerging market stocks is so expensive that an index fund often wins on a net basis. And if you're using a taxable account, remember the higher taxes that come with high portfolio turnover.

WEIGHTING YOUR PORTFOLIO

When you combine different subasset classes, you need to decide not only which to choose, but also in what proportion. Example: You've decided your portfolio should have 70 percent stocks, 25 percent bonds, and 5 percent short-term bonds. Your next step is to decide what *kinds* of stocks and bonds you want and *how much* of each. At this point, you'll need to choose a method of "weighting," which specifies how much of your money should go into each subasset class. There are a variety of ways to do this, each with its own advantages and disadvantages (see chapter 14).

MPT PORTFOLIOS

If you'd like to explore the potential of a portfolio constructed according to modern portfolio theory (MPT), you have several choices. With a healthy six-figure amount to invest, you can contact a financial planner or one of the major brokerage operations.

Some of these sources have the specialized software needed to create an MPT portfolio.

Another way is to consider a risk-controlled set of global index funds. Quantidex, for example, consists of five global indexes, each designed to provide maximum return for a fixed level of risk. Originally meant for employers with tax-advantaged plans, the Quantidex management style is now available to individuals. It takes the form of five blends of index funds, each representing a different level of estimated risk and return. A Quantidex fund requires a minimum investment of $100,000. Quantidex indexes are monitored by Morningstar, the Chicago investment research company. Detailed quarterly statements are available, but not the range of services offered by large fund families. Source: Daniels & Alldredge Investment Management, Birmingham, AL: 205-323-4000.

MALKIEL'S INDEX FUND PORTFOLIOS

In chapter 14, Malkiel shows his sample portfolios. What you'll see is three fully diversified portfolios consisting entirely of index funds and balanced by age group.

Superficially, they may seem similar to portfolios you can find in hundreds of other sources. The difference is, those portfolios do not necessarily reflect the ideas described in this book. These do. They are not only all-index fund portfolios; they also reflect basic principles such as asset class rotation and the kind of diversification implied by Modern Portfolio Theory. *They are the essence of this book translated into actionable information.*

Deadline investments

There are times when you have to have a specific amount of money at a specific time. If you want to finance a home, you need the money by a certain date. The same applies to college expenses. The money has to *be there* when you need it. Depending on the length of time, this may call for different tactics from those used for retirement. Here are two kinds of investments that meet the need:

CERTIFICATES OF DEPOSIT

A common way of dealing with a deadline is to buy bank certificates of deposit (CDs). When a current certificate matures, you roll it over into a new one, and so on, until you need the money. Upside: Your money is protected by the Federal Deposit Insurance Association. Downside: You have to pay taxes on the interest even though you don't get it. The rate may be low compared with another alternative. If you withdraw the money before the term of the certificate, you pay a stiff penalty.

ZERO COUPON BONDS

What may be a better way, depending on your situation, is something called "zero coupon bonds." This is a bond that pays nothing during its term; you get all the money (principal plus interest) when the bond matures. Upside: If you buy U.S. Treasury zeroes, you are *absolutely guaranteed* to get all the money you expect on the maturity date. And the rate you earn is usually higher than the CD rate. Downside: You have to pay income tax on the interest you earn each year, even though you don't collect it. Also, zero coupon bonds are extremely volatile when they are years away from maturity. The best way to buy them is directly from discount brokers, such as Jack White (800-233-3411) or Waterhouse Securities (800-934-4443).

Caution: Although CDs or zeros are a good way to invest for a special purpose, they should not be your only way. All the principles we've discussed, including the need for diversification and balance, still apply. Deadline investments can be a relatively large part of your portfolio when you need the money in just a few years. Otherwise, you may be better off with the kinds of stocks and bonds we've discussed.

SUMMARY

- You don't invest with individual stocks, bonds, or mutual funds. You invest with a portfolio. The portfolio is your investment tool.
- Deciding how much risk to take is a key issue. Age and time frame are good measures, but the best guide is the level implied by your financial plan.
- By referring to the seventy-year history of the major asset classes, professionals can estimate future returns (which imply estimated risk levels) for a variety of model portfolios.
- According to the studies we reviewed in chapter 8, the percentage of money you have in stocks, bonds, and cash will determine the vast bulk of your risk and return.
- There are at least six ways to buy or build a portfolio. Your choice depends on a variety of factors, including the kind of investor you are: None of It Myself, Some of It Myself, or All of It Myself.
- Malkiel's portfolios, detailed in chapter 14, crystallize the most important ideas discussed in this book, including the superiority of index funds, asset class rotation, and Modern Portfolio Theory.
- Deadline investments, such as zero coupon bonds, can be useful in certain situations.

CHAPTER 12

Giant Step 4:
Cut Taxes

PICTURE PEOPLE WHO CAN BARELY SWIM STRUGGLING IN COLD water and yelling for help. Sailors on a nearby boat toss out life preservers. But the people in the water refuse to take them. They just keep complaining about how cold the water is. This is similar to what many Americans are doing about taxes on their investments: They aren't using the life preservers the government offers. Which brings us to:

GIANT STEP 4: TAKE ADVANTAGE
OF INVESTMENT TAX BREAKS

Take full advantage of every investment tax break that makes sense. Do this before you put a cent into taxable investments.

Many people are perfectly willing to invest lots of time in trying to identify hot stocks or mutual funds. And yet, many of these same people invest very little time in trying to minimize taxes on their investments. Taxes are tedious, aren't they? Not nearly so much fun as imagining you might win big in the roulette game of Pick-a-Hot-Fund. Which brings up the prospect of people feverishly pursuing the highest returns while failing to max out on their 401(k). Or not setting up a Keogh. Or not contributing to a Roth IRA. *The irony is, minimizing your investment taxes could bring you a higher return than even the hottest mutual funds.* Let's look at how you can do that—taxable investments first and then "tax-advantaged" (tax-deductible and/or tax-deferred).

> *Important:* This section is not intended to provide professional tax counsel. The idea is simply to give you an overview of what's out there, so you'll know what questions to ask your accountant or tax attorney.

TAXABLE INVESTMENTS

Taxes on investment earnings have strategic importance. As we saw earlier, a fund's *after*-tax return can be a lot less than its published, *pre*-tax return. John C. Bogle, The Vanguard Group chairman and founder, gave a telling damage report when he spoke to a professional group in November 1997. Drawing on an article in *The Journal of Portfolio Management* by Jeffrey and Arnot, Bogle said:

> *By the end of 25 years, the government has consumed 47% of the optimal ending dollar amount, while the manager pocketed 12%, leaving the investor with only 41% of the investment on an after-tax, after cost basis. And it is the investor who put up 100% of the initial capital.*

Sort of clarifies the message, doesn't it? For taxable accounts, you have to consider potential taxes when you build your portfolio, especially if you're in a high tax bracket. As mentioned earlier, this means focusing on (among other things) a fund's *turnover* (how often it buys and sells securities). To give you a benchmark, the average diversified stock fund has a turnover of 85 percent; the average stock *index* fund comes in at less than 5 percent. (Small Cap and emerging market index stock funds may be slightly higher.) So the index fund generates far less in the way of distributed capital gains.

Another way to reduce the impact of taxes on your investments is to *buy and hold*—and put your money in funds that buy and hold. That way, you *defer* capital gains, instead of *paying* capital gains taxes. Which again brings us back to index funds. Buy and hold is the name of their game.

You can also cut taxes by investing in *tax-managed funds.* Offered by big mutual fund companies, these funds follow several practices aimed at holding taxes to a bare minimum, consistent with a good growth rate. For investors in medium to high tax brackets, they're worth a close look.

TAX-ADVANTAGED INVESTMENTS

Tax-deductible and tax-deferred accounts are one of the most effective ways to increase the net return on your investments. Yet most salary-earning Americans are not contributing the maximum amount to their 401(k) or 403(b) plans—and a high percentage has not even joined an available plan. Let's see what they're missing (and hope you're not among them).

Your friend, the IRS

I'm serious. The IRS taketh away, but it also provideth. For decades, Congress has tried to encourage saving and investment.

It's part, they say, of our American heritage—the idea that every adult should stand on his or her own feet, instead of being dependent on some form of Big Brother. So various laws offer investment tax breaks, including the Taxpayer Relief Act of 1997. Here are some of those tax breaks, old and new.

DEFINED CONTRIBUTION PLANS LIKE 401(K)S

For most people, this is the largest sum of money they will ever accumulate. To refresh your memory, the 401(k) applies to employees of profit-seeking businesses; the 403(b), to nonprofit organizations. With either one, the amount you contribute is definite, but not the amount you receive; that depends on how well your portfolio performs. Defined contribution plans offer four tax breaks, plus a big advantage unrelated to taxes:

1. The amount you contribute is *tax-deductible*. Let's say you earn $100,000 a year, and your plan allows you to contribute 15 percent of that to your account. In the eyes of the IRS, this reduces your taxable income to $85,000. This puts you ahead in two ways: You don't pay federal income tax on the $15,000 that goes into your account. And depending on your tax bracket, the tax saving liberates money you would otherwise have paid the IRS—money you can now invest. Over time, that extra amount can make a big difference in how much your account grows.

2. The accumulated earnings in your plan are *tax-deferred*. That means you can postpone taxes on both the income and the capital gains earned by your plan. (Income, if you'll remember, comes from stock dividends and interest payments; capital gains come from increases in the value of the funds in your plan.) You do have to pay taxes on any amount you withdraw from your plan. But if all goes well, that won't be until you retire, when you may be in a lower tax bracket. In any event, tax-deferral puts more yolk in your nest egg.

3. Many employers, especially large companies, match their employees' contributions, at least up to a point, often in the form of company stock. This is as close to "free money" as you're ever likely to get. A typical arrangement is for an employer is to contribute half as much as the employee up to a dollar limit. This is valuable in itself. Beyond that, the IRS says the employer's contributions are also tax-deferred, just like the amount you contribute.

4. The limit on contributions to a plan goes up with increases in the cost of living. In 1998 the limit was about $10,000. These increases are also tax-sheltered.

The big advantage beyond tax savings is automatic investing, which we looked at in the chapter on retirement. Again, you're much more likely to save and invest if the money never comes into your hands. Through thick and thin, your trusty defined contribution plan just keeps socking it away, giving you the benefits of dollar-cost averaging and the power of compounding.

In brief: If your employer adds to your plan, the amount you contribute is *multiplied five ways:*

1. Tax-deductible contribution
2. Tax-deferred growth
3. Your employer's contribution (also tax-deferred)
4. Your investment return (income plus capital gains)
5. The relentless effects of compounding

Shelter even more: If you're in a 401(k) or 403(b), but have independent income from other work—consulting, for example—the bountiful IRS allows you to shelter your separate income through a separate plan.

Add it all together, and you've got a tax-advantaged bonanza. You'd think practically everyone would grab as much of this deal as possible. You'd be wrong. According to the Employee Benefits Research Institute, 36 percent of U.S. workers are not in any kind of employer-sponsored plan. And a stunning 63 percent of those in a 401(k) are not contributing the maximum amount. What a waste.

MAKING IT BETTER

Good as your plan is, there are at least two things you can do to make it better. One involves the choice of funds. Typically, an employer hires one of the big fund families or an investment management firm to set up customized portfolios. In any case, employees often wind up with a choice of a half-dozen or so non-index funds. Good, but not good enough. Many defined contribution plans don't offer index funds. This is bad. We've shown that index funds are likely to perform better and more reliably than their non-index counterparts. *You should have that advantage available to you.* But there's a hitch. The fund families and investment managers make very little profit on index funds. So there's little incentive to offer them.

Costs are another problem. Employers don't pay them. You do. And the costs are hidden in the machinery of the plan. Some employers are zealous about holding those costs to a minimum. Others are not. Obviously, it costs money to administer a defined contribution plan, and it's fair that you pay these costs. But in many cases, the costs are excessive. The reason: Since the employer doesn't pay them—and you don't know what they are—there's no disinterested third party policing the amount charged. (SEC, are you listening?) An article in the September 1997 issue of *Bloomberg Personal* observes:

> *The result of this cozy little partnership* [between mutual fund companies and employers]: *Mutual fund fees in 401(k) plans are roughly double what they should be, according to Adele Langie Heller, director of defined contributions consulting with Rogers Casey in Darien, Connecticut.*

The article quotes another professional, who describes the situation in more colorful language:

> *"There is real pillaging going on," says William McNabb, head of the institutional business at the Vanguard Group in Valley Forge, Pennsylvania. "There are funds that charge [about 2 percent]. That's egregious. Participants should scream."*

The May 1998 issue of *Money* has a cover story entitled "What's Wrong With Your 401(k)." I'll just give you a few of the subheads:

"Limited choices, poor returns."
"You're in the dark."
"Fees keep climbing."
"You get too much company stock."

Looking ahead, the money in your 401(k) or 403(b) could be the single, largest amount of wealth you're going to accumulate. It's vital to make sure your plan gives you everything the law allows. To get this issue of *Money*, call 212-522-2275.

ONE WAY TO TAKE ACTION

Considering the index fund issue and the cost issue, you could have a situation that demands immediate action. Here are a couple of suggestions on what to do:

1. Petition your employer to add a variety of index funds to the menu of options. (See the following "Request for Change" form.)
2. In a separate action, ask for information about costs.

This is not blue sky talk. Remember why your employer has a defined contribution plan in the first place. Your company wants to hold on to its valued employees, and the plan offers a relatively low-cost way to give you a considerable financial benefit. *In short, your employer wants you to be happy with your plan, or it's a waste of money.* That fact can be very helpful in persuading your employer to improve the plan.

In addition, index funds (depending on legal interpretation) may be better for your employer. Since they don't require a plan sponsor to select superior subjective management, they may lighten the company's due diligence burden.

To make things easier for you, I've drawn up a request form you and your co-workers can duplicate and sign.

REQUEST FOR CHANGE IN
DEFINED CONTRIBUTION PLAN
A message to the Human Resources Department

As employees of this company, we are grateful for the defined contribution plan that management has generously provided. We realize it is not required by law and that it represents a valuable source of additional compensation, with major tax advantages. At the same time, we have a suggestion on how to make the plan even better:

Include index funds in a wide range of asset classes, for at least three reasons:

- *Index funds have performed better than the average non-index fund in a wide variety of asset classes.* They are likely to continue this superior performance because of inherent advantages over non-index funds.
- *Studies show that past performance does not reliably predict future performance.* This means employees cannot expect to outperform index funds simply by choosing non-index funds with a history of above-average gross returns.
- *Index funds have proved more reliable than the average non-index fund.* They are protected from the risk of poor

judgment by investment managers. Properly structured, they will track closely the performance of the asset classes they represent. This is a strong advantage, considering the importance of the plan to our peace of mind and future financial security.

For these reasons and more, we who have signed below ask that index funds in a variety of asset classes be added to the plan's menu of investment options. Please advise us of your response to this request.

(Signatures)

MUNICIPAL BONDS

Believe it or not, the ever-generous IRS offers even more tax relief, provided you're in a relatively high tax bracket. Municipal bonds are exempt from federal income taxes. Depending on where you live, they may also be free from state and local income taxes (triple tax-free).

The idea behind this benefit is to lower the cost of borrowing for state and local governments. Since the bonds are tax-exempt, issuing agencies can offer less than the going rate for similar taxable securities and still attract investors. For example, if your taxable income is $100,000 on a joint return, you could buy municipal bonds paying only 4 percent and probably do just as well as if you bought a taxable bond paying 6.5 percent. The latter figure is called an "equivalent taxable yield," referring to the break-even point between tax-exempt and taxable bonds. The exact point depends on variables that only your accountant knows for sure.

Like taxable bonds, municipals come in varied degrees of risk and times to maturity—from one or two years to twenty-five years. Fortunately, you can buy municipal bond *funds*, to gain the benefit of diversification. Most of the big mutual fund companies have a wide range of municipal bond funds to suit your needs. To lower risk, you can buy funds consisting of *insured* municipal bonds. This means the bonds are insured as to timely payment of interest and principal. They are *not* insured against any loss that results from changes in price, and they pay a slightly lower rate of interest than uninsured bonds.

A better bond: There's a special kind of tax-exempt bond called "AMTs" (short for alternative minimum tax). They're not attractive to the fortunate few who have managed to shelter a large part of their income, because these bonds are subject to the alternative minimum tax. But for the rest of us not in that enviable position, AMT bonds are a good deal. They pay about .2 percent more than regular bonds.

Caution: Municipal bonds can change in market value, up or down. Be sure to make them part of a diversified portfolio that includes a high proportion of index funds. Also, since all municipals are free from federal income taxes, there's no point in putting them in a tax-deferred account.

And now we move on to a major event in the history of investment taxes.

THE TAXPAYER RELIEF ACT OF 1997

Not content with the blessings of defined contribution plans and municipal bonds, Congress provided a package of additional tax breaks in the Taxpayer Relief Act of 1997. The act covers investments, education, buying and selling homes, and estate matters. We'll focus on the part about investments (enough for a book in itself).

Before we get into this topic, I have to tell you it's complicated. I've made it as simple as I know how—even to the point of leaving out a lot of points—and it's still complicated. But you need to know this stuff, so bear with me and I'll try to get us through it with a minimum of fog. The story centers on two main benefits: lower, more democratic capital gains taxes, and new and improved IRAs. Let's take them in that order:

1. Lower, more democratic capital gains taxes

The new tax law bestows a double benefit: First, it makes capital gains tax rates available to everybody, regardless of tax bracket. Second, it lowers the rate for long-term capital gains from 28 percent to 20 percent. A welcome exception is that people in the lowest tax bracket pay only 10 percent.

Originally, the law created a new system of "holding periods": short-term, mid-term, and long-term. But that was too complicated even for Washington. In August 1998, the law was mercifully amended (retroactive to January 1, 1998) to provide only two holding periods:

- *Short-term:* If you realize your gain during a period of twelve months or less, the gain is treated as ordinary income. You pay up to 39.6 percent, depending on your tax bracket.
- *Long-term:* If you realize your gain during a period of more than twelve months, you pay (at the most) 20 percent, instead of the previous 28 percent.

The holding periods apply to everyone. The rates do not. If you're in the 15 percent bracket, you pay lower rates: 15 percent for short-term gains, 10 percent for long-term gains. Dividend income and interest income are still taxed at the same rate as ordinary income

2. New and improved IRAs

Individual retirement accounts (IRAs) were created by Congress to give the vast majority of taxpayers the right to build a tax-advantaged account simply as individuals. You don't have to work for a company or own a business. Depending on your income, you may be entitled to an IRA even if you're in a 401(k) or 403(b).

Before the Taxpayer Relief Act of 1997, IRAs were a good way to shelter some of your income. The new law makes them even better in at least three major ways:

1. It creates two new kinds of accounts to make IRAs a better deal for more people (*Roth* and *Education*)
2. It allows *both* members of a couple to contribute to their own IRA (subject to conditions)
3. It raises the qualifying income limits, making IRAs available to more people

That's a quick overview. Now let's get down in the grass.

TRADITIONAL IRA (DEDUCTIBLE)

This is the good old IRA you know and love. Only now, it's even better. Under the new law, each member of a couple can contribute up to $2,000 a year to his or her own IRA, even if both members are covered by an employer plan (subject to income limits). The great thing about this kind of IRA is that you can *deduct the contribution* to your account from your income (provided you don't earn more than a specified amount). As far as the IRS is concerned, that money doesn't exist. On top of that, the earnings from your account grow tax-deferred. And if you're *not* covered by an employer plan, you can deduct and shelter up to $2,000 a year, regardless of how much you earn.

Downside: Your withdrawals are taxed as ordinary income, even the long-term capital gains. For people covered by an employer plan, the income limits for a $2,000 deduction are relatively low—an adjusted gross income (AGI) of $30,000 for singles and $50,000 for couples. And you must start withdrawals no later than age 70½.

TRADITIONAL IRA (NON-DEDUCTIBLE)

This IRA is for people who earn too much to qualify for a deductible IRA. It gives you the benefit of tax-deferred growth, regardless of how much you earn. This can make a big difference in how much you accumulate.

Downside: As the name implies, your contributions are not tax-deductible. Part of your withdrawals are taxed as ordinary income. And you have to begin withdrawing money at age 70½.

ROTH IRA

This new IRA (named after the senator who sponsored it) addresses the tax downside head on. If you meet certain conditions, your withdrawals are free of federal taxes. The ever-generous IRS will levy no federal taxes on the money you withdraw, provided you're at least 59½ and have held the investments at least five years. A Roth has higher income limits than traditional IRAs—$95,000 for singles and $150,000 for couples. Also, you never have to take money out of a Roth, not even after you're seventy years old, which makes it a good tool for estate planning.

Downside: Your contributions to a Roth IRA are *not* tax-deductible. But for many people, that disadvantage is far outweighed by tax-free withdrawals and other advantages. Like traditional IRAs, Roth IRAs have income limits.

A better deal for families

The new tax law raises the amount a couple can shelter. The new limit is now $2,000 per year, *per person,* even if both are covered by a plan at work. That's total of $4,000 a year. This applies to both traditional and Roth IRAs. Because of compounding, the higher limit more than doubles the rate at which couples can accumulate tax-advantaged earnings. Income limits apply.

Higher income limits

The 1997 law raises the maximum income limits to qualify for an IRA. The rules are complicated and depend on a variety of variables, mainly the Adjusted Gross Income on your federal income tax form. Consult your tax advisor.

Traditional versus Roth

What's clear so far is that a valuable tool to shelter income from taxes has been substantially improved. But now there's a decision you never had to make before: "Which way should I go? Traditional or Roth?"

The answer (as usual) depends on your situation. Roth IRAs have generated a lot of excitement. Financial writers have used words like *fantastic* and *huge opportunity* to describe it. And, in fact, it's the best choice for some people. For example, if you're young, affluent, and have an ongoing investment program destined to reach seven figures, go with a Roth. The bigger your nest egg (and the younger you are), the more you'll save by not having to pay taxes on your gains. As mentioned, the same feature makes it a good tool for estate planning, since you're not forced to take out money at any particular age. Your heirs can continue to get income that's free of federal income taxes.

On the other hand, a Roth may not be for most people. Using the license of brevity, here's how it shapes up:

- If you're in a *higher* tax bracket after you retire, a Roth clearly gives you a better deal.
- If you're in the *same* tax bracket after you retire, it gets more complicated. Depending on certain variables, a traditional IRA will give you a higher *gross* amount. But when you factor in taxes, a Roth may give you a higher *net* amount.

- If you're in a *lower* tax bracket after you retire—and especially if you're down to 15 or 18 percent—the traditional IRA is likely to be your best choice.

Hold on. In the retirement chapter we learned that financial planning models assume a *lower* income after retirement. That brings up a question: What percent of taxpayers will be in the same or a higher tax bracket at that point in their lives? The 1995 *Statistical Abstract of the United States* (115th edition) says that the median income of people aged fifty-five to sixty-four is $33,474. For those aged sixty-five or more, the figure drops to $17,751. The median is the point where half the people are above and half below. If the median income drops by almost 50 percent after retirement, there can't be a high percentage of people who move to a loftier tax bracket when they retire. After all the fanfare, it may be that the good old-fashioned IRA is the best deal for most people.

Other topics: Keep in mind that we haven't covered expanded withdrawal rights (including those for physically challenged people and first-time home buyers), IRAs for education, rollovers from a traditional IRA to a Roth IRA, and many other topics.

For more information: Most of the major mutual fund companies have booklets and/or computer software dealing with IRAs. One example: the T. Rowe Price Analyzer disk for $9.95. T. Rowe Price also offers a free IRA newsletter with work sheets (800-401-4644).

Tax-wise tactics

Money maker: The IRS lets you wait until April of the following year to make your IRA contribution for the previous year. You'll do better to make your contribution as early as possible in the year for which you're paying taxes. That way, you defer more income than if you wait until the following year.

Tax cutter: When you sell shares from a taxable account, sell the shares you've held for more than eighteen months first, so you can get the low rate for long-term capital gains.

IRA Rollover

The IRS, in its endless beneficence, understands that people change jobs, so it offers a way to transfer your retirement plan from one place to another. You can "roll it over" into a new retirement plan without losing a cent, *provided* you meet certain conditions. The simplest way to handle a rollover is to have your old employer send a check or wire transfer payable to your new plan provider. It must cite your name and account number or social security number.

On the other hand, your old employer may give you a check made out to you. In that case, you have sixty days to deposit the money in a rollover IRA. Otherwise, the IRS, despite its legendary magnanimity, will do terrible things to you. Don't even think about letting that happen. Talk with your tax advisor, or contact one of the big mutual funds companies or fund supermarkets. Most of them have a booklet dealing specifically with rollovers.

Tax-deferred variable annuities

Whether tax-deferred variable annuities make sense depends a lot on where you buy them.

We'll get into that. But first let's make sure you know what we're talking about. A tax-deferred variable annuity is one or more mutual funds wrapped in a life insurance policy and sold as a package, which the IRS allows to grow tax-deferred. It's called "variable," because your results are not guaranteed by the insurance company; they depend on the performance of the funds in the annuity. The total package has advantages and disadvantages:

WHAT'S GOOD
* Your money grows tax-deferred. Under the right conditions, that can give you a considerably larger nest egg than a taxable account.

- There's no limit on the amount you can invest.
- If you die, your heirs are guaranteed to get the market value of your holdings, or at least the amount you invested, whichever is greater.

WHAT'S BAD

- If you buy your annuity from a typical source (a brokerage operation or a financial planner operating on commissions), the cost is prohibitive. Sales commissions grab 5 percent to 7 percent; operating expenses run to more than 2 percent. Add those costs, and you're looking at a giant-sized ball and chain.
- When you start drawing on your account, the IRS says it's all ordinary income, even the capital gains. That was always a problem with annuities. Now, with the new tax law, it's even worse; you can't get the benefit of the lowered rate for long-term capital gains. (This is also true of employer plans.)
- Typically, there are severe penalties for withdrawing money in the first few years—or for withdrawing more than 10 percent in any twelve-month period until you reach a stipulated age (usually 59½).
- If, despite all the evidence, you decide to choose funds based on their past performance, you're in even worse shape than usual. A fund's performance dates from when it started, almost always as the mutual fund equivalent of a baby. As part of an annuity, you get into the fund *after* it's grown up. So don't expect the performance of the funds in your annuity to match the performance record of the same funds outside the annuity.

WHAT'S RIGHT

This is a no-brainer: It doesn't pay to buy annuities from an individual planner or salesperson. The costs are so high, it can take decades to equal the return of the same funds in a taxable account.

On the other hand, there is such a thing as a *no-load* tax-deferred variable annuity. There are even no-loads with low operating costs. Buying these annuities could make a lot of sense, provided:

- You're at the legal maximum with all other tax-deferred accounts, including 401(k), 403(b), IRA (Roth or regular), Keogh, and so on.
- You intend to use the annuity as a long-term investment—at least ten years, preferably more.
- Average operating costs for funds in the annuity come in at less than .5 percent—no need to pay more.
- You're in a medium to high tax bracket. Otherwise, the disadvantages may outweigh the benefits.
- You're sure you won't have to make large withdrawals during the term of the contract.

Don't let these criteria put you off. If you meet them, a no-load, low-cost variable annuity can be an excellent investment. The tax-deferral works like a multiplier for growth, and the lack of limits on contributions allows you to shelter more money than you could in any other way. Three sources for no-load, low-cost annuities: Charles Schwab (800-435-4000), T. Rowe Price (800-469-5304), The Vanguard Group (800-523-0352).

So far, we've been talking about *variable* annuities, where your results depend on how well your funds perform. There's also a *fixed* annuity that provides dollar-definite payments guaranteed by an insurance company. These are designed mostly for retired people who want to make absolutely sure they'll have a certain minimum income.

If you're self-employed

Displaying its usual empathy, the IRS understands that not everybody is an employee. It offers a range of plans for self-employed people to shelter their retirement savings. Typically, you can shelter *more money* in these plans than in the employee-oriented plans we just reviewed. The most popular plans for self-employed people include:

SIMPLIFIED EMPLOYEE PENSION (SEP-IRA)

The big advantage of these plans, besides the tax benefits, is their simplicity. You don't need a degree in accounting to understand how they work. They're designed for sole proprietors, partnerships, independent contractors, small corporations, or any other self-employed person.

KEOGH PLANS

These are more complex than SEPs, but they have certain advantages. The main one: You can shelter *even more money.* Some types of Keogh plans allow you to shelter up to $30,000 a year.

Putting it all together

If you're very lucky, you may have a high-class problem. You may be "maxed out" on tax-advantaged plans—and still have money left over, perhaps from an inheritance or sale of a second home. If you don't buy an annuity, you'll have to set up a taxable account. The result could be several different accounts, some taxable, some tax-advantaged. Follow this prescription to minimize the pain of taxes:

- *Use your taxable accounts* for municipal bond funds and growth stock funds. The bonds aren't subject to federal income taxes, so you lose nothing. Growth stocks tend to pay low dividends, so you don't lose much.
- *Use your tax-advantaged accounts* for taxable bond funds and high-dividend stock funds. Without the tax advantage, these types of funds would generate a significant amount of taxable income.

Caution: As you do that, don't lose sight of your appropriate asset allocations; they take precedence over optimal tax moves. Fortunately, you can usually do both. Also, be sure to treat all your accounts as a single portfolio. For example, the total of all the bond funds in *all* your accounts should add up to the percentage called for in your investment plan. The same goes for subasset allocations.

SUMMARY

- Giant Step 4 calls for taking full advantage of every tax break that makes sense—*before* investing in taxable investments. This means contributing the legal maximum to tax-advantaged accounts—401(k), 403(b), IRA, self-employed and small business plans, and (maybe) a no-load, low-cost tax-deferred annuity.

- Taxes on investment earnings have strategic importance. For people in the higher tax brackets, they can lower net returns by 50 percent or more.

- Four ways to minimize investment taxes: Use tax-advantaged accounts for all they're worth. Buy and hold. Buy index funds (low turnover rates). Buy tax-managed funds.

- Defined contributions plans are extremely valuable. Make every effort to be fully invested in your plan, especially if the employer matches part of your contribution.

- Good as they are, defined contribution plans can be improved by adding index funds to the range of fund choices. Ask your employer to do that. Also, participants should learn about the cost of non-index funds in their plan; they're likely to be too high.

- Individual Retirement Accounts (IRAs) are an effective way to shelter some of your income from taxes. The new tax law makes them even better.

- The 1997 Taxpayer Relief Act (among other things) liberalizes several features of the traditional IRA. It also creates a new kind of IRA (Roth), which is usually a better deal for people who retire with the same income or a higher income than they had before retirement.

- Tax-deferred variable annuities may be a good choice if you meet certain criteria, but many have prohibitive costs. It pays to buy them from no-load, low-cost sources.
- The federal government allows a variety of tax-advantaged plans for self-employed people. Generally, they permit higher contributions than those allowed for employees.

(This chapter was reviewed by the CPA firm Jason Maxwell, Ltd., Scarsdale, New York.)

CHAPTER 13

Giant Step 5:
Don't Tinker, Don't Wait

W E'VE SEEN WHAT HAPPENS WHEN FUND MANAGERS AND
other Great Predictors try to time the markets: Short of
getting lucky, they can't do it. Neither can investors. Yet they
keep trying—and keep losing money.

The pressure to change your portfolio when the markets
make a big move in either direction is enormous. When you see
the value of your portfolio declining week after week (or month
after month), a strident voice yells in your ear, "Don't just sit
there. *Do* something." Similarly, when you see an asset class
soaring upward, and you're not in it, the urge to rush to the
phone is all but overwhelming. This is especially true if you have
a friend who *is* in it, and, of course, tells you how wonderful it is.

Even worse than bragging friends are financial publications
and newsletters. You read an absolutely convincing article on why

energy stocks are bound to take off (or keep taking off). You read a trenchant explanation of why midcap value stocks will rule the markets. Another article explains why, in painful detail, bonds will do better than stocks. All these authors are certified experts; you're not. Whom should you believe? The correct answer is to ignore them all: Stay the course with a portfolio that reflects your financial and investment plans. But that's easier said than done. We're all subject to basic drives that tend to rule the markets:

1. *Greed* (we try to out-guess the markets by buying when we think they'll go up)
2. *Fear* (we sell when we think the markets may go down; or, perhaps even worse, we intend to develop an investment program like the one described in this book, but we decide to wait until the time seems right)

Both of these practices are serious mistakes. They can cost you a lot of money, not to mention living with long-term regrets along the lines of, "How could I have been so dumb?" All of which leads us to

GIANT STEP 5:
BUY AND HOLD,
STARTING NOW

Let's begin with a counterintuitive idea. Suppose a mutual fund goes up 45 percent in two years. Common sense says investors in the fund saw the value of their shares rise by the same amount. Sounds right, but it's not. The only investors who made 45 percent on their money were those who got in at the start and held their shares for the full two-year period. Typically, most investors get in too late and sell too early. An especially valuable study by Dalbar, Inc., the Boston research company, makes the point:

Investment return is far more dependent on investor behavior than on fund performance.

What *you* do is more important than what the markets do. This is a Big Idea, which is why it's Giant Step 5. You can be certain of getting the same return as a fund (or asset class) *only* if your buy and hold. Possessed by fear and greed, investors try to improve their results by market timing. On average, they fail miserably. The same Dalbar study reports:

Trading in mutual funds reduces investment returns. A simple buy and hold strategy outperformed the average investor by more than 3 to 1 over the 12-year period studied.

Picture this in neon lights: *Buy and hold produced a three-to-one advantage.* The evidence is clear. Once you have an appropriate portfolio, the most productive thing you can do is nothing. That's true until there's a major change in your financial situation, or when price movements throw your asset class percentages substantially out of line. In the second case, it may be prudent to rebalance your portfolio to get back to your specified asset allocation, keeping a wary eye on the tax consequences. These small adjustments should not be confused with market timing.

The value of buy and hold has been documented many times. H. Bradlee Perry, a consultant and former chairman of David L. Babson and Company (Cambridge, Massachusetts) went at it from a different point of view. He compared bull markets with bear markets, with these results:

- The average bear market is relatively short—about eight months, with full recovery in slightly more than a year.
- Rallies happen quickly and in big jumps.
- The most harmful risk investors face is not bear markets, but missing out on bull markets.

Notice that last point. Earlier we saw that the fear of losing money is stronger than the desire to make money. So your instincts are apt to lead you astray. In the real world, the loss from missing a rally is usually greater than the loss from being caught in a down market. Remember that for the past seventy years, the S&P 500 has moved up in three years out of four.

I know the wisdom of buy and hold from personal experience. It was early in 1996, after a year in which the S&P 500 zoomed up 37 percent. Market valuations (price-dividend, price-earnings, book value) were way out of line with historical averages. I got nervous, so I called an investment manager (George Daniels, Daniels & Alldredge, Birmingham) for advice. Here's what he said:

> Don't get out of stock funds, because if you do, you won't know when to get back in.

I took that advice and made many thousands of dollars. I invite you to do the same. On top of that there's the tax factor. When you try to time the markets, you are likely to generate capital gains distributions—and capital gains taxes.

MORE ON MARKET TIMING

The title of an article in the October 1996, issue of *Smart Money* says it all: "Perfect Timing Is Still Bad Timing." The heart of the article is a comparison between two investors. During a five-year period from 1989 through 1994, one times the market perfectly, buying at the lows and selling at the highs. The other simply hangs in there. The results are enlightening:

> The market timing would have impressed your friends, but not your accountant. That's because of the 28 percent federal tax on capital gains. The bill comes to . . . 10 per-

cent of the portfolio. That's worse than anything the market did to the investor who rode it out.

As mentioned, the new tax law reduces the tax on *long*-term gains to 20 percent and continues to tax short-term gains (twelve months or less) at ordinary income rates. So the outcome of this study today might be different, but not by much. The article goes on to point out that the "real world" result would be even worse because of state income taxes, sales loads, and commissions. These items, the author says, could "easily eat up 40 percent of your gain—or about 20 percent of your entire portfolio."

THE ANTIDOTE: INVEST AUTOMATICALLY EVERY MONTH

We touched on this point in the chapter on retirement. But now we're going to come at it from a different point of view. Most investment professionals agree that the best way to invest over the long term is by a process called "dollar cost averaging." This refers to investing the same amount every month, *regardless* of how the markets have performed recently.

It works like this: By investing the same amount every month, you buy more shares per dollar when prices are down and fewer shares when prices are up. As a result, the average *cost* of your shares will be less than the average *price* of those shares over the same period of time.

The idea of regular monthly investment is more than just another technique to close the Money Gap. It's probably the single most effective way to make a big difference in the amount you accumulate. Among the advantages:

- Deals with the frailty of human nature ("I want a new car now, not later")
- Takes full advantage of the power of compounding

- Gives you the benefit of dollar cost averaging
- Keeps you from trying to time the markets, a crime that often brings harsh punishment

The combined weight of these points adds up to a major advantage. Regular monthly investing is not just a good idea; it's something you can't afford not to do.

WHEN TO START INVESTING

This is easy. Start investing as soon as you've decided how to structure your portfolio and where to buy the ingredients—and do those things as quickly as possible. The penalties of waiting are severe. The rewards are great. This follows from the arithmetic of compounding and the growth of global economies and stock markets.

The Vanguard Retirement Investing Guide, described earlier, provides a good example: Two people of the same age contribute to a company plan and earn the same rate of return. Over the years, Rita contributes $25,000; Steve, $10,000. Whom do you think winds up with the larger amount after thirty-five years? Steve earns $80,200; Rita, only $67,700. How can that be, when Rita contributed over twice as much? I didn't tell you a vital fact: Steve started 10 years earlier. Time can be more important than money.

One last example comes from the July 8, 1997, issue of *Pensions & Investments.* They report on a study by the Consulting Group (a Smith Barney division) in Wilmington, Delaware. The headline tells the story: "No wrong time to invest, study finds."

Reporting on six different time periods from 1940 to 1995, the study found investors earned a good return (more than treasury bills, more than inflation), even if they invested only at the worst possible times—at a series of peaks in the S&P 500.

WHY DO WE WAIT?

Clearly, it pays to make time your friend, not your enemy. But even people who know that may find it hard to take that last, vital step. The are all kinds of reasons to procrastinate:

- *"I'll be in a better position to do it later."* With all due respect, you probably won't. There's always a reason not to make a major move with most of your assets. It's scary. But the passage of time will not make it less scary.
- *"I'm not sure I've made the best possible choices."* This is letting perfect be the enemy of good. Wisdom calls for getting an appropriate portfolio in the first place. You can always refine it later.
- *"The markets are too high."* The truth is, you don't know if the markets are too high or not. As we've seen, nobody can predict the markets. Overwhelmingly, the hard evidence says you're likely to do best if you invest as soon as you have your financial and investment plans.

STATUS REPORT

We've come a long way. From believing in fancy fund managers to believing in index funds. From buying things that sound good to being guided by financial and investment plans. From believing in individual stocks, bonds, and mutual funds to believing in asset class rotation and diversified portfolios, balanced to fit your needs. From trading driven by fear and greed to the steady course of buy and hold. All these changes will help you earn more and sleep better.

CHOOSING A
MUTUAL FUND FAMILY

Congratulations. The big moment has arrived—you're primed and ready to act. But where do you buy? It depends on what you want. If you prefer to delegate the whole process to someone else, see chapter 9. Short of that, you need to choose one or more mutual fund families.

It's convenient (but not vital) to deal with a single mutual fund family. You see your whole portfolio on one consolidated statement; you can make transfers among funds with a simple phone call; and tax accounting becomes simpler.

If simplicity is your goal—and if you want to invest with a full range of index funds at the lowest possible cost—there are at least two obvious choices: Charles Schwab and Vanguard. Both offer a package of index funds that gives you broad coverage of the global stock and bond markets. If you're interested in certain subasset classes, it's worth remembering that Schwab has four index funds and Vanguard, twenty-three. The fund supermarkets (see below) also sell index funds. At Fidelity's supermarket, for example, you can buy four in-house stock index funds and a Dreyfus diversified bond index fund.

But number of funds is not the only point to consider. What about things like breadth of services, Web sites, and account statements? In its September 1997 issue, *Smart Money* published the results of its own survey of fifteen leading mutual fund companies. Each company was rated on five criteria and given numerical scores. *The study was service oriented; fund performance was not considered.* Top-of-the-line results for seven companies:

Fidelity	42.5	800-544-8888
Vanguard	40.3	800-662-7447
Janus	38.1	800-525-8938
Scudder	36.9	800-225-2470

American Century	34.0	800-345-2021
T. Rowe Price	33.9	800-638-5660
Dreyfus	33.8	800-645-6561

Fidelity won out with its range of services, while Vanguard beat the pack in quality of customer service representatives. To get numerical scores, *Smart Money* had to quantify some things that are hard to quantify. Still, the results may be a useful guide. To order this issue of *Smart Money:* 800-925-0485.

For a comprehensive list of all kinds of mutual funds (twenty-four pages worth), divided by asset class, see Burton Malkiel's *A Random Walk Down Wall Street.* He cites eleven points of information for each fund, including sales charges, expense ratio, and ten-year annualized return.

FUND SUPERMARKETS:
THE PROS AND CONS

Some people prefer to deal with "fund supermarkets." These are discount brokers that sell hundreds or thousands of different funds—many with no sales charges or transaction fees. Something for nothing? Not quite. According to an article in *Mutual Funds* (November 1997), the supermarkets charge the funds from .25 percent to .4 percent for taking them on board. This cost is passed on to customers in the form of higher expense ratios. For a bond index fund, for example, you might pay .6 percent, instead of .2.

The big advantages of supermarkets are choice and convenience. You have access to thousands of funds (and stocks) with a single phone call. You get a consolidated statement, and it's easy to transfer among fund families.

Supermarkets work best for active investors who buy a mixture of individual stocks, bonds, non-index funds, and index funds. Courtesy of the *Mutual Funds* article mentioned above, here are the top five supermarkets ranked by the number of participating fund families:

Jack White	800-233-3411
Fidelity	800-544-9697
Charles Schwab	800-435-4000
Dreyfus	800-843-5466
Waterhouse	800-934-4443

A ranking by dollar volume would put Schwab on top and Fidelity second. If you're seriously considering a supermarket as your source of non-index funds, you might want to get a copy of this *Mutual Funds* article: 800-442-9000.

There are also on-line supermarkets. Two examples: E*TRADE (www.etrade.com) and Lombard (www.lombard.com). They tend to have lower transaction fees.

SPREADING THE WORD

I've always believed you don't know something until you can explain it to somebody else. Let's assume you're having lunch with a friend, and he or she wants to know how you invest. In a situation like this, you need short, simple points you can keep in your head. The conversation might go like this:

"You're in index funds? What are they?"

"An index fund is a group of stocks or bonds that have something in common, for instance, whether they're big companies or small companies."

"So what's the point?"

"Well, if you look at big-stock index funds for the last fifteen years, they've beaten about 90 percent of non-index funds."

"Ninety percent. Sounds good. But what about the other 10 percent? Why not buy those instead of index funds?"

"Because you don't know what they'll do in the future."

"Who says so?"

"Economists. They've studied this subject to death, and they all have come up with pretty much the same conclusion: Long term, there's no practical way to beat the markets by betting on past performance."

"I don't get it. The people who run these funds—they're all pretty smart."

"Right. But non-index funds have much higher costs than index funds. Also, they tend to have sales charges and higher capital gains taxes. On a net basis, you're a lot better off with index funds."

"You mentioned big stocks. Suppose I want to buy different kinds of stocks and bonds."

"No problem. You can buy an index fund for practically any type of security."

"Is that what you did—buy different kinds of index funds?"

"Yeah, I got a portfolio that fits my situation. So I'm in on whatever's going up, and don't get hurt too much when the markets go down."

"Speaking of which, how safe are index funds?"

"They're more reliable than non-index funds. You always do as well as a particular market, and you don't have to worry about your fund manager making a blunder."

"So, you just buy a mixture of index funds and wait for the market to go up."

"Not exactly. I started with a financial plan to see how much I needed to invest. Then I got an investment plan, which told me how to divide up my money into stock funds and bond funds."

"And that's it?"

"No. I've maxed out on my 401(k), and we put $4,000 a year into IRAs. The tax advantage makes a big difference."

"Well, it all sounds like something to think about."

"Sure, but don't think too long. You know about the effects of compounding. The sooner you start on a better way to invest, the more money you'll make."

*   *   *

Okay, I admit your lunch companion was a little too easy. Still, I think this conversation shows how you can cover the essence of this book—in simple language—in a few minutes. And when you can do that, you *own* the message. That's a big deal. You've earned the right to earn more and sleep better. Read Burton Malkiel's closing chapter—especially his sample portfolios—and you're ready to go.

IN A WORD

When I completed this portion of the book, I wondered if there was any ultimately simple way to sum up its message. I believe this is it:

Confidence.

This book is all about trading the hope of spectacular gains in return for confidence that we will meet our long-term goals. As confident investors, we avoid the chancy business of trying to predict the future price of individual securities or mutual funds; we invest in index funds. We don't pretend to know the future darlings and pariahs of the market; we're diversified to prepare for whatever might come. We have no illusions about timing the markets; we buy and hold.

We invest with confidence.

CHAPTER 14

An Update on Index Funds, with Model Index Portfolios

B Y NOW WE HOPE YOU ARE CONVINCED THAT INDEX FUNDS should be the cornerstone of your portfolio. But index funds are the Rodney Dangerfield of mutual fund investments—they seldom get respect, whether from financial writers hyping the "hottest" fund, or from securities brokers selling you products on which they can earn the highest sales commissions. Over the years, brokers have told me repeatedly that index funds guarantee mediocre returns—or, even worse, that they are unpatriotic. Indeed, most brokers paid by sales commissions will not even mention index funds to their customers. But during the late 1990s, investment professionals have raised a new set of concerns about index funds—concerns that need to be addressed head-on.

IS THE SUCCESS OF
INDEXING SELF-FULFILLING?

The latest rap against indexing is that it is self-fulfilling and ulti-mately self-defeating. The argument goes something like this. In-dex funds that mimic the Standard & Poor's 500 stock average have been extremely popular in recent years. The inflow of in-vestment dollars into these funds has, it is alleged, boosted the prices of S&P stocks and has led to the self-fulfilling result that S&P index funds have widely outperformed active managers. The result, according to critics, is that the S&P is now bloated with vastly overpriced stocks and will ultimately come crashing down much like the "nifty fifty" stocks of an earlier decade.

It is important first to point out that despite the increased popularity of indexing, the impact of indexing is still small rela-tive to the general flow of funds into the equity market. Indexed equity mutual funds comprise less than 6 percent of all equity mutual funds. Even during 1996 and 1997, years of increased popularity of indexed equity funds, less than 15 percent of the net cash flow into equity mutual funds went into S&P 500 index funds. Moreover, institutional investors participate more in in-dexing than individuals do, and there does not seem to be any in-crease during the 1990s in the share of institutional assets that are indexed according to surveys conducted by Greenwich Associ-ates. It is therefore implausible to suggest that an increase in the popularity of indexing has had a self-fulfilling effect on the rela-tive performance of the S&P 500 index versus the rest of the stock market. Moreover, the popularity of S&P 500 indexing during 1996 and 1997 could not have been responsible for the superior performance of the 50 largest stocks in the S&P 500 versus the other 450 stocks in the index since the impact should have been the same on all 500 stocks. Thus, the success of indexing can hardly be explained by its growing popularity with individual investors.

By way of review, here are some of the major points we have made in previous chapters. Index funds have regularly produced rates of return exceeding those of active managers by about 2 percentage points. There are two fundamental reasons for this excellent performance: management fees and trading costs. Public index funds are typically run at a fee of .2 percent. Actively managed (non-index) public mutual funds charge annual management and market expenses that on average are 151 basis points (1.5 percent) per year. Moreover, index funds trade only when necessary, whereas active funds typically have a turnover rate approaching 100 percent, and often even more. Using very modest estimates of trading costs, such turnover probably costs the active manager at least another .5 percent to 1 percent of performance a year, and probably more. Even if stock markets were less than perfectly efficient, active management as a whole cannot achieve gross returns exceeding the market as a whole and therefore managed funds must, on average, underperform the indexes by the amount of their expense and transactions costs disadvantage.

From 1994 through 1997, almost none of the active managers had beaten the S&P 500 index, and the advantage of the index has been considerably wider than usual, especially compared with the 1991 to 1993 period. There are, I believe, two explanations for this recent performance of index funds relative to active managers.

First, the S&P index, while a substantial part of the total market, represents a particular stratum of the securities available for investment. As my co-author Richard Evans has noted, the S&P 500 is a large-company index. The top fifty companies in the S&P represent about 50 percent of the weight of the index. (The S&P index is a capitalization-weighted index, which means that bigger companies whose capitalization, or equity value, is large get a bigger weight in the index.) Over the long run, according to data by Ibbotson Associates, small companies have produced rates of return exceeding those of the S&P 500 index of larger firms. But during periods when large companies have done especially well, as has been the case in the mid-1990s and beyond, one should expect the relative advantage of the index to increase. The reason is that actively managed (non-index) funds tend to hold a wider set of securities, including those of smaller capitalization firms, which in this period have performed less well.

Index funds also should have a relative advantage during sharply rising markets. Because these funds are designed to track their chosen index, they do not hold a cash position or, if they do, the position is balanced by an offsetting futures position. Actively managed funds, however, typically carry a cash position for liquidity that may at times be as high as 5 percent to 15 percent of the fund's net asset value. Thus, when the market rises sharply, as it did in the mid-1990s, the advantage of all index funds (including even funds that use a broader index than the S&P 500) should increase.

I have run a statistical test to explain the degree to which S&P 500 index funds beat the average equity manager during the 1980s and 1990s. My results were unambiguous. Index funds increased their advantage during sharply rising markets and when large stocks outperformed small stocks. Moreover, there was no relationship between the quarterly flow of funds into index funds and the performance of these funds. Finally, I found that active managers appear to have increased the proportion of large-company stocks in their portfolios during the mid- to late 1990s. Thus, it was not simply S&P 500 index funds that had been buying the large S&P stocks during this period. Active managers had been buying the same stocks as well.

It appears that indexing is not a pernicious practice that has done particularly well since the mid-1990s because of a self-fulfilling rush toward indexing on the part of investors. Indexing has regularly and consistently acquitted itself against active managers, and the unusually large benefits of S&P 500 indexing during the mid-1990s are the logical and expected consequence of ebullient markets, especially for large-cap stocks. While S&P

500 indexing is likely to lose some of its advantage during down markets and in markets where small-cap stocks outperform the stocks of larger companies, the expense and transactions costs advantage of indexing will continue to serve investors well. Index funds should continue to outperform non-index funds even in bear markets.

A BROADER LOOK AT INDEXING

For all the attractions of indexing, there are valid criticisms of too narrow a definition of indexing. As Evans has emphasized, indexing should not be equated with a strategy of simply buying the S&P 500 index. It may well be that the extraordinary performance of large-cap domestic stocks that dominate the S&P 500 will not continue and that the long-run superiority of small-cap stocks will reassert itself. Over most of the twentieth century, smaller companies have generated larger rates of return than big companies. Moreover, many traditional financial analysts argue that better values often exist in these smaller companies, or in international stocks, or in real estate equities. As Evans notes, however, index funds currently exist that mimic the performance of various Wilshire, Russell, and other indexes of small-cap stocks, the Morgan Stanley Capital Index of European and Australian and Far Eastern (EAFE) securities, emerging markets securities, and real estate investment trusts (REITs). These index funds have also tended to outperform actively managed funds investing in similar securities, as will be explained below. In addition, bond index funds are available that have also outperformed managed bond funds.

For example, the graph on page 249 compares actively managed international funds with the MSCI (Morgan Stanley Capital International) indices of European and Japanese securities. While more than half of actively managed Japanese funds did beat the index over a three-year period ending on December 31,

1997, only one-third beat the index over a five-year period. Over a ten-year period ending in 1997, none of the actively managed U.S. mutual funds investing in Europe beat the Morgan Stanley index.

Indexing also can be a useful strategy even in emerging foreign markets. One might think that the case for indexing would be weaker in the relatively less efficient and less well followed stock exchanges in emerging markets. But, paradoxically, it is precisely the relative inefficiency of emerging markets that makes indexing pay here as well. Actively managed emerging-market funds have management fees and other expenses that are far greater than for developed markets. While many actively managed funds did beat the index during 1997, not one non-index emerging-market fund beat the MSCI Emerging-Markets Index during the first half of the 1990s. Moreover, the transactions costs of buying and selling in these markets are likely to be several times as large as is the case in developed markets. Also, a variety of stamp taxes and fees makes trading costs very expensive in these markets. It is also the case that index funds have done well compared with non-index, small-cap stock, bond, and real estate investment trust (REIT) mutual funds.

There are strong reasons to build a portfolio that branches out from the S&P 500. Diversification—even into very risky securities such as those in the high-growth emerging markets of the world—is a time-honored technique that can smooth out portfolio fluctuations and allow investors to sleep much better at night. As Evans has carefully explained in chapter 8, diversification can actually allow investors to add risky holdings to their portfolios in a way that offers both higher returns as well as lesser overall portfolio risk. It sounds contradictory but actually, it's a profound insight. Today, modern portfolio theory is routinely taught in economics departments and business schools around the world and used by most professional investment managers to improve portfolio performance.

The trick is to find combinations of securities whose returns are

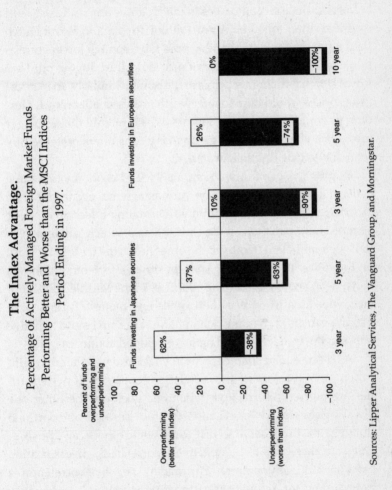

The Index Advantage.

Percentage of Actively Managed Foreign Market Funds Performing Better and Worse than the MSCI Indices Period Ending in 1997.

Sources: Lipper Analytical Services, The Vanguard Group, and Morningstar.

not highly correlated. Thus, when one market or industry goes into a tailspin, the results are cushioned by stability, or even positive developments, in other markets. For example, a portfolio consisting of Toyota and Nissan Motors is highly, or positively, correlated since all companies in the Japanese auto industry tend to rise and fall together. A portfolio of Toyota and Royal Dutch Petroleum, on the other hand, would have a much lower correlation. An increase in the price of gas could hurt Toyota but help Royal Dutch with higher prices at the pump. Similarly, an increase in gas prices would hurt Toyota, which makes smaller cars, far less than it would hurt General Motors, which mainly makes bigger cars, since when gas prices go up many consumers prefer to buy more fuel-efficient, smaller cars.

In practice, even in an integrated world economy, the same events have different effects on various national economies. The oil crisis of the 1970s had a more devastating effect on oil-poor Europe and Japan than on the United States, which is at least partially self-sufficient in oil. On the other hand, the tenfold increase in the price of oil had a very positive effect on Indonesia, Venezuela, and oil-producing countries in the Middle East. Similarly, increases in mineral and other raw-material prices have positive effects on nations rich in natural resources and negative effects on manufacturing in many developed countries.

As discussed in chapter 8, the key factor in whether diversification can reduce risk is the correlation coefficient. If two securities are perfectly correlated (when one goes up, the other one always goes up), diversification will not smooth out portfolio fluctuations. But if some securities zig while others zag (the securities are then said to be negatively correlated), diversification can virtually eliminate risk. Fortunately, negative correlation is not required for diversification to work its risk-reducing magic. All you need is for individual securities to be less than perfectly correlated. The good news for investors is that correlations between index funds of various national markets are sufficiently low that diversification can reduce risk considerably. While times of great distress are likely to affect all markets negatively for a short period of time, over the longer run national markets tend to be much less synchronized.

Moreover, real estate equities, as would be available in real estate investment trust (REIT) index funds, tend to have quite low correlations with general stock prices. Also, bonds and stocks often move in opposite directions, particularly during periods of recession and financial crises. Thus, a portfolio that is diversified both internationally and domestically, with small and large stocks, and that includes other asset classes, such as real estate and bonds, is likely to serve investors far better than one more narrowly focused on one domestic index such as the S&P 500 index. As mentioned, index funds are available to allow investors to access all these kinds of securities at low expense and in a tax-efficient manner.

HOW INDEXES
ARE CONSTRUCTED

The next issue may strike the reader as rather technical, but it has important implications for individuals trying to decide how to allocate their assets over a variety of index funds. It is important information for investors who want to earn more while sleeping well. I will explain how indexes are constructed, what they actually contain, and why it matters.

Capitalization-Weighted Indexes

Most indexes are capitalization weighted. The capitalization of a company is measured by taking the price of its stock and multiplying by the number of shares. The index gives a weight to each stock based on its capitalization. Suppose the index is made up of two stocks: stock A selling at $20, with one million shares outstanding, and stock B selling at $10, with two million shares outstanding. If stocks A and B have the same capitalization (in this case they do, since both have a capitalization of $20 million), then the index will reflect a simple average of the market values of the two stocks. But if A has a capitalization of $12 billion and B has a capitalization of only $1 billion, then the stock A will get twelve times the weight of B in the index. The Standard and Poor's 500 stock index is capitalization weighted. The biggest companies, such as General Electric, do not get 1/500th of the weight of the index. In fact, GE gets about 1/40th (2.5 percent) of the weight of the index because of its large size. Moreover, the fifty largest companies in the S&P 500 get about one-half the weight of the index.

Equal-Weighted Indexes

An alternative weighting scheme would give each stock contained in the index an equal weight. Thus, an equal-weighted S&P 500 index would give each stock in the index an equal weight of 1/500th or .2 percent. The index is actually calculated by assuming that an equal number of dollars is invested in each of the stocks and then calculating subsequent values of the portfolio after prices change. Under this scheme all five hundred stocks in the index would have equal influence as opposed to the actual S&P 500, which gives substantially more weight to the largest firms.

Price-Weighted Indexes

Perhaps the most popular index is neither equal-weighted nor capitalization-weighted. The index is the Dow Jones Industrial Average of 30 Stocks and it is price-weighted. Thus, stocks that sell at a very high price get most of the weight in the index. Suppose initially there are three stocks in the index and they sell at prices of $90, $60, and $30 respectively. The index is calculated by adding up the three prices and dividing by three. The index then would stand at $60. Now suppose the $90 stock went up 10 percent to $99 and the other two stocks were unchanged. An equal-weighted index would show a gain of 3.3 percent reflecting the fact that (only) one-third of the portfolio had a 10 percent gain. Note, however, that the price-weighted index would go up 5 percent from 60 to 63 [(99 + 60 + 30)/3 = 63]. What has happened is that the higher priced stock has more influence than the lowest price stock. (If the $30 stock was the only one that went up 10 percent to 33, the index would only rise to 61 [(90 + 60 + 33)/3]).

PROS AND CONS OF DIFFERENT METHODS OF CALCULATING INDEXES

Price-Weighted Indexes

While price-weighted indexes are very popular—the Dow 30 is often equated with how the market is doing—such indexes have several flaws that can present problems for use as the basis of index funds. One flaw of a price-weighted index is that high-priced shares with small capitalizations will have a larger index weighting than low-priced shares with big capitalizations. In addition, most price indexes are based on a narrow list of stocks and, therefore, may not be as representative of the market as a whole as larger indexes. Finally, it turns out that when a stock splits and has a lower price, its weight in the index gets reduced. If a fund tried to mimic the index, it would have to sell some of the split shares and place the money raised in all of the other constituent shares. The transactions costs and potential tax liabilities involved present problems for a price-weighted index, such as the Dow 30. For these reasons, most index funds are capitalization weighted. The Dow 30 Industrial Average does include the largest and most successful multinational corporations headquartered in the United States, however, and it has enjoyed an excellent long-run performance. Investors can buy a Dow Jones

30 Industrial Index Fund from some mutual fund families. There are also traded Dow 30 index securities. These are called Diamonds and they are listed on the American Stock Exchange. They can be purchased in the open market through any broker, and they tend to have lower expense ratios than the Dow 30 mutual funds.

Equal-Weighted Indexes

Historically, at least until the mid- to late 1990s, an equal-weighted S&P 500 stock index has outperformed the actual cap-weighted S&P 500. For many years, the stocks of smaller companies generated somewhat higher rates of return than the stocks of larger companies. This is why some analysts have favored an equal-weighted index over a cap-weighted index. The critical disadvantage, however, is that the basket of securities in the index fund would need to be continuously rebalanced in order to keep the shares in the fund weighted equally. Transactions costs would increase enormously, as would potential tax liabilities, obviating some of the major advantages of indexing.

Capitalization-Weighted Indexes

As mentioned above, most index funds are based on capitalization-weighted indexes, such as the S&P 500 or the Wilshire 5000. In principle, a broad cap-weighted index presents the best representation of the market as a whole and the entire investable universe of equity securities. The Wilshire 5000 index, for example, represents more than 99 percent of the total capitalization of the entire U.S. equity market. Moreover, the major advantage of capitalization-weighted indices is that no rebalancing is required when different components of the indices change weights because of market movements. For example, suppose that because of capital appreciation, the weight of IBM in the index rises from 1.5 percent to 2 percent. Since the index fund simply holds onto its IBM stock, the increased weighting of IBM in the index fund will occur automatically. (A price-weighted index fund will also automatically increase the weight accorded to IBM, but the weight would be lowered in the event IBM split its shares.) While there will be a slight amount of buying and selling required as stocks enter and leave the index, such turnover is likely to be extremely small.

For all the advantages of capitalization-weighted indices, however, such indices are not perfect. Since a cap-weighted index is based on market prices, it tends to increase the weight of components whose stocks have recently done well. As a result, it could lead investors to increase their exposure to stocks or markets where prices could be under the influence of some kind of speculative craze. A recent example of the experience of indexed investors in developed international markets will clarify the point.

As mentioned above, the major index of developed overseas stocks is compiled by Morgan Stanley Capital International (MSCI) and is popularly known as the EAFE index, where EAFE stands for Europe, Australia, and the Far East. The weights in the index are based on the market weights of all the available stocks in each market. During the late 1980s, the Japanese stock market experienced an extraordinary rise that was widely interpreted as a speculative bubble. The stock market doubled and then doubled again with P/E ratios approaching 100, far in excess of anything experienced in Japan's financial history. As the prices of Japanese stocks rose, so did the weight of Japan's market as a percentage of the EAFE index. Investors who bought the EAFE index found that almost two-thirds of their portfolios were invested in overpriced Japanese stocks. Had the index been weighted according to the relative sizes of the constituent countries' economies (as measured by their total output or gross domestic product [GDP]), Japanese stocks would have been limited to about one-third of the index. Thus, investing in an index that is market-value weighted will not protect an investor from being overinvested in precisely those stock markets experiencing a speculative mania. During the 1990s, the Japanese stock market crashed, losing almost two-thirds of its value at its low point. We shall see in the specific recommendations that follow how we can at least partially correct for such an overweighting by adjusting the proportions of individual capitalization-weighted indexes.

In addition, some emerging-market indices, which are based on the total market value of the investable stocks of each country, may not represent the relative sizes of the component countries. For example, China is the largest emerging market in terms of its total output of goods and services, yet it had a very low weight in the MSCI emerging-markets index during 1997. In addition, in many foreign countries such as Japan, some companies own a significant portion of the shares of other companies. The problem in such a case is that the capitalization of the market will be affected by double counting. In other countries, the government owns a large fraction of the shares of many companies, and the market's total capitalization will overstate the amount of stock available for investment by the public.

In our specific recommendations that follow, we will generally use capitalization-weighted indexes because they best represent the low-cost, buy-and-hold strategy we have recommended in this book. But we will make some adjustments to the cap-weighted indexes to correct for some of the biases noted above. The adjustments that we will recommend will be described in the following section.

SOME SUGGESTED
INDEX-FUND PORTFOLIOS

Let's first review the main lessons of this book. Index funds should constitute the core of any sensible investor's portfolio. Index funds sharply reduce management fees, transactions costs, and taxes. Index funds typically outperform actively managed

"Dilbert" reprinted by permission of United Feature Syndicate, Inc.

funds even before considering taxes, and their performance advantage grows significantly over time. These funds tend to be broadly diversified and are generally less risky than actively managed funds. Individual investors are finally learning what professionals have known for years: Indexing leads to improved investment results. No investors should be in the position of the Dilbert character (figure 9) of not knowing what index funds are and what their advantages are.

But indexing does not mean simply limiting yourself to the largest U.S. companies that comprise the Standard and Poor's 500 stock index. There is a time-honored investment principle of not putting all your eggs in one basket—even if the basket contains the largest and best U.S. companies. Broad diversification reduces risk. Portfolios should contain not only large blue-chip companies but dynamic, newer small companies as well. Moreover, portfolios should be diversified internationally as well as domestically and should also contain other asset classes such as bonds and real estate. Fortunately, a variety of index funds offer investors an opportunity to participate in the rewards of indexing in many different stock, bond, and real estate markets.

One further principle of personal finance needs to be reviewed before we get to specific recommendations. As Evans has mentioned earlier, younger people have a greater capacity for risk than older individuals, especially those who have begun retirement and are looking for income to sustain their lifestyle. Young people can count on their earnings from employment to sustain them during periods of stress in world stock markets. Moreover, the younger you are, the more time you have to ride out the characteristic ups and downs of the stock market and the more likely you are to obtain a satisfactory rate of return from riskier assets. Hence in the recommendations that follow, the thirty-year-old is advised to shoot for higher returns and is assumed to be willing to accept a riskier and more volatile portfolio. Thus, relatively safe short- and long-term bonds make up only 20 percent of the recommended portfolio and substantial amounts of the portfolio are placed in more volatile common stocks, such as those of smaller companies and from emerging markets where growth opportunities (as well as risks) are larger.

The sixty-five-year-old is assumed to be nearing (or perhaps already in) retirement. The recommended portfolio has over 50 percent invested in bonds and real estate equities, which are not only far less volatile securities but also throw off substantial income during the year to be used for living expenses. Retired individuals do not usually have earnings from employment to cushion any reverses in the stock market. Hence, only 10 percent of the portfolio is placed in riskier small-cap and emerging-market stocks. But even those in retirement need some equities for potentially generous returns as well as diversification, so the core of the portfolio is placed in an S&P 500 index fund (and there is some representation of smaller companies and stocks in developed and emerging foreign markets). Note that the recommendations for the "aging baby boomer" retain a substantial equity exposure but begin the process of moving to a relatively safer retirement type of portfolio.

Now a few words about the specific funds recommended in the exhibit below. All the funds are index-type funds and all have very low expenses. For most categories I have given a choice of funds. Readers should know that I am a director of The Vanguard Group of Investment Companies, the mutual fund complex that pioneered indexing for the public investor. I have tried to recommend non-Vanguard funds where they meet our low-expense criteria. In some cases, however, such as real estate investment trust (REIT) funds and emerging-market funds, I have listed only the Vanguard fund because it is the only index fund available.

While there are other (EAFE) index funds investing in developed foreign markets, I have recommended the Vanguard funds for some of the reasons mentioned earlier in this chapter. The capitalization-weighted EAFE index can in some circumstances significantly overweight some economies relative to the size of their economic activity. Hence, the weighting recommended is 60 percent for the European part of the EAFE index and 40 percent for the Japanese and other public sector. These weights roughly correspond to the gross domestic product (GDP) weights of the various economies. Vanguard is the only mutual fund complex that splits up the parts of the index so that one can partially correct for the potential biases in the EAFE index. While the Vanguard emerging-market index is not perfect from the standpoint of the weighting of its component parts, it does somewhat reflect liquidity characteristics and is well diversified. Individuals may want to adjust the recommendations toward or away from more volatile equity investments depending on their attitude toward risk. In general, one can expect a somewhat higher rate of return from higher risk investments.

Note that these recommendations generally use capitalization-weighted index funds because they tend to have fewer disadvantages than index funds constructed in any other way. But we have recommended specific weights for the components of the portfolio. These components have been derived from an MPT statistical analysis such as that described in chapter 8. Thus, the portfolio is very widely diversified both internationally and among asset types so as to keep risk as low as possible consistent with the return that is sought.

Two questions need to be addressed at this point. First, suppose an investor starts off with a portfolio balanced as suggested but after a few years the weights no longer correspond to those in the table because some markets have appreciated more than other markets. What's an investor to do? For example, suppose emerging markets rebound sharply in the portfolio designed for the thirty-year-old and the weight in the portfolio shifts from 10 percent to 15 percent. My advice is to sit tight. Frequent rebalancing will involve paying capital gains taxes and your portfolio will still be very well diversified with slightly different percentages. But suppose now that the emerging market share rises to 25 percent. Here I would pare back a bit and not allow any component to be more than twice the recommended weight. The proceeds from any sales could be placed in an underweighted component. You will find this rule is unlikely to force you to do much trading at all, but it does guard against being seriously overweighted in stocks that may be involved in some speculative bubble (as was the case in Japan in 1989).

Another question may well be on the minds of investors with very little cash. Most mutual funds have a minimum investment requirement (although they tend to be less restrictive for IRAs and for other retirement plans). You may not be able to buy all the recommended components. No problem. Start with a broad-based U.S. index fund and start adding the other components as your resources increase. (See table on page 262.) Indeed, for a U.S. stock index fund you might want to use the Vanguard Total Stock Market Index Fund, a fund that has both large and small stocks, because it mimics the Wilshire 5000 index. Later you can add other components, and most investors tend to build up their stakes by making periodic investments over time. There is no need to do everything at once. In fact, since younger investors are likely to be adding resources to their portfolios over time, any rebalancing that might be desirable can often be accomplished by putting any new cash to work in the underweighted components of the portfolio.

A FINAL COMMENT

Whatever asset composition you choose, you will earn more and sleep better if you build your portfolio with index funds. Compared with actively managed funds, your risk will be lower, your net returns after expenses will be higher, and you will pay far less in taxes (to the extent your investments are held outside of tax-favored retirement plans). Indexing is a winning investment strategy whose recent growth reflects not a passing investment fad, but the realistic adjustment of individual investors to one of the not-so-well-kept secrets of the investment business—there's no way any portfolio manager can consistently beat the market. The wave of indexing is now only in its infancy. In a few years, most intelligent individual investors will use index funds as the core of their portfolios.

SOME SAMPLE INDEX PORTFOLIOS

Percent Invested			Index Fund	Telephone Number of Fund Company	Expense Ratio
30-year-old saving for retirement; willing to accept price volatility	Aging baby boomer in late 40s; still willing to accept considerable risk	65-year-old retired; need for income; very risk averse			
25	25	25	Fidelity Spartan Market Index Fund (S&P 500)	800-544-3902	.19%[1]
			or		
			T. Rowe Price Equity Index Fund (S&P 500)	800-638-5660	.40%
			or		
			Vanguard Index 500 Fund	800-662-7447	.19%
15	10	5	Charles Schwab Small Cap Index Fund	800-435-4000	.38%
			or		
			Merrill Lynch Small Cap Index Fund	800-637-3863	.75%
12	10	6	Vanguard EAFE European Portfolio	800-662-7447	.31%
8	7	4	Vanguard EAFE Pacific Portfolio	800-662-7447	.35%
10	8	5	Vanguard Emerging Markets Portfolio	800-662-7447	.57%

			Fund	Phone	Expense ratio[1]
10	13	15	Vanguard REIT Index Fund	800-662-7447	.36%[2]
15	22	30	Vanguard Total Bond Market Portfolio _or_ Merrill Lynch Aggregate Bond Index Fund	800-662-7447 / 800-637-3863	.20% / .60%
5	5	10	Vanguard Short-Term Bond Fund _or_ Charles Schwab Short-Term Bond Index Fund	800-662-7447 / 800-435-4000	.20% / .38%

[1] All funds are "no-load," but in order to defray transactions costs there are the following purchase fees:

Fidelity Spartan Market Index Fund: 0.5% redemption fee (for shares held < 90 days); $10 annual index account fee if investment < $10,000. (The symbol "<" means "less than.")

Vanguard Index 500 Fund: $10 annual fee.

Charles Schwab Small Cap Index Fund: 0.5% redemption fee (for shares held < 6 months).

Vanguard EAFE (both European and Pacific Portfolios): 0.5% purchase fee; $10 annual fee.

Vanguard Emerging Markets Portfolio: 1% purchase fee; 1% redemption fee; $10 annual fee.

Vanguard REIT Index Fund: 1% redemption fee (for shares held < 1 year).

Vanguard Total Bond Market Portfolio: $10 annual fee.

Vanguard Short-Term Bond Fund: $10 annual fee.

[2] This is an estimated expense ratio during the fund's first year of activity.

INDEX